Hermann and Alexander Lauer

The Shirt
Making-Design-Pattern

About the authors

Hermann Lauer was born in 1947. After apprenticeship to salesman in textile industry, he
has practical course in weaving and finishing
of fabrics and apprenticeship in tailoring with
Master degree. He owns a diploma as a model
maker and fashion designer.
He works since 1974 for famous clothing companies in Germany, UK, Turkey
Since 1996 he is product manager for German
shirt companies and production supervisor in
Eastern Europe and Asia.

Alexander Lauer, was born in 1969.
After apprenticeship as a salesman for retailing
and a long term practical work experience, he
specialised for organization with emphasis on
computer technology and quality management.
Since 2001 he is self employed consultant for
the textile industry.

The authors are very grateful to their close friend Sue Thomas for proofreading

© 2007 Hermann and Alexander Lauer
Cover design: Alexander Lauer
Drawings: © 2007 Hermann and Alexander Lauer
Translation: Hermann and Alexander Lauer

Printing and production: Book on Demand GmbH, Norderstedt, Germany

ISBN 978-3-8334-8488-9

Contents

Contents

Contents

Contents

Contents

Introduction

Preface

This Book is not based on scientific or theoretical research, but it was written with our work experience, so this publication can be used as a practice orientated guide.

After 30 years working in the clothing industry, first as a designer, model and pattern maker, later as travel technician and product manager the authors decided to document this long-term experience.
Also teaching in various fashion colleges – Düsseldorf, Hannover, Hamburg and London – was a massive influence to publish this book, to give students insight into the garment industry and to help them, to start a career in this important and interesting section of the textile industry.
This book can also be a reference for buyers, staff in charge of quality standards and product managers, as well as for designers, technicians and students of fashion and textile technique.
It could also be interesting for fashion journalists, retailers or interested amateurs. This is the reason why we gave up the normally used technical terminology.
Each company has its own production documents and internal know how. But there was no book written which contains all areas from design and pre production, preparation to manufacturing and quality management.

We wish you a pleasant and informative reading.

Hermann and Alexander Lauer

Section overview

Part 1 Introduction

Section overview
In this section we will describe:

- Types of shirts
- Pattern parts of a shirt
- Fabrics
- Interlinings
- Seams and sewing threads
- Button and buttonholes
- Other details
- Other accessories and presentation

Types of shirts

Types of shirts

Synopsis

We can classify shirts into the following categories, according to the use for different occasions. The lines are fluid and can overlap.

Term	Occasion	Characteristics
Evening or Smoking shirt	Festive events like marriages, opera galas and others.	Long sleeve, exclusive fabrics, mostly in colour white, rarely ecru, covered fly front placket, without pocket. It is worn with bow tie or black tie.
Formal tailored and business shirt	Professional appointments and meetings, worn in combination with a classic suit.	Top quality, very formal executive and business shirt with a "handtailored character" in solid classic fabrics and colours, rarely with stripes. Long sleeve. Kent or Shark fin collar, one pocket, worn with a correct tie.
City dress shirt	Dress shirt for job (offices, banks, etc.) where correct appearance is important, but also for free time.	Mostly long sleeve, in summer season also short sleeve possible. Fabrics fine weaves e.g. fil - á – fil, chambray, pastel colours and stripes. Correct collars but not too stiff, chest pocket, worn with tie. The shirt is less formal then a business shirt.
Semi-dress shirt	More fashionable shirt for informal jobs and leisure time.	Long and short sleeve, fabrics in all qualities, patterns like stripes and checks or plain. Collars are Kent, New Kent and Button-down. Collars and cuffs are softer fused, shirt can be worn open without a tie.
Casual shirt, also crash and washer shirt	Informal shirt for travelling, weekend and leisure time.	Easy, relaxed shirts with soft handle e.g. in cottons, linen, mixed materials, flannels, with patterned fabrics like checks, stripes, etc.
Fancy shirt	Informal shirt for holidays, beach and parties.	Made in soft materials and handle, design with pattern and prints; wellness is important but not form stability.

Types of shirts

Costume shirt	Formerly part of national costumes, today it is a casual shirt with costume influences and details.	Long or short sleeve, sometimes roll-up sleeve; often rustic looking fabrics and materials (e.g. linen or linen mix), real horn or mock horn buttons, embroideries and decorative accessories. Design follows examples from Tyrolean or sometimes maritime character (e.g. Fishermen's shirt).
Uniform and service shirt	Part of service clothing or uniforms e. g. pilots, army, police, train conductors, etc.	Long and short sleeve, mostly with two chest pockets, often with pocket flap. Shoulder flaps fixed with loop or small tunnel and button to show the rank of the wearer. Materials are e.g. poplin in solid colours; the colour has to follow service regulations. Service shirts express corporate identity.
Working or guild shirt	Part of work- wear, traditionally worn by craftsmen like carpenters, butchers, cooks, chimney sweepers, miners and others.	Long or short sleeve, colour and form follow tradition or identities and rules of the profession. Made in robust materials e.g. canvas, corduroy, etc.

Components of a man's shirt

Components of a man's shirt

Synopsis

In general a man's shirt consists out of the following components, which are also part of the set of patterns:

- Left (over wrap)and right front part (under wrap) with front fastening (placket)
- Back part with back yoke
- Sleeves
- Collar
- Also parts which are added or left out depending on design of the shirt
- Special components (e.g. Epaulettes)
- Cuffs for long sleeves
- Sleeve plackets (sleeve guards)
- Pockets
- Pocket flaps

Further important components of a shirt

- Interlinings
- Seams and hems
- Top stitching
- Buttons
- Trimmings and accessories
- For components with decorative character see chapter „Design"

In the following chapters the different pattern parts and other components will be described in detail regarding general points, measurements, measuring areas and manufacturing advise.

Types of shirts

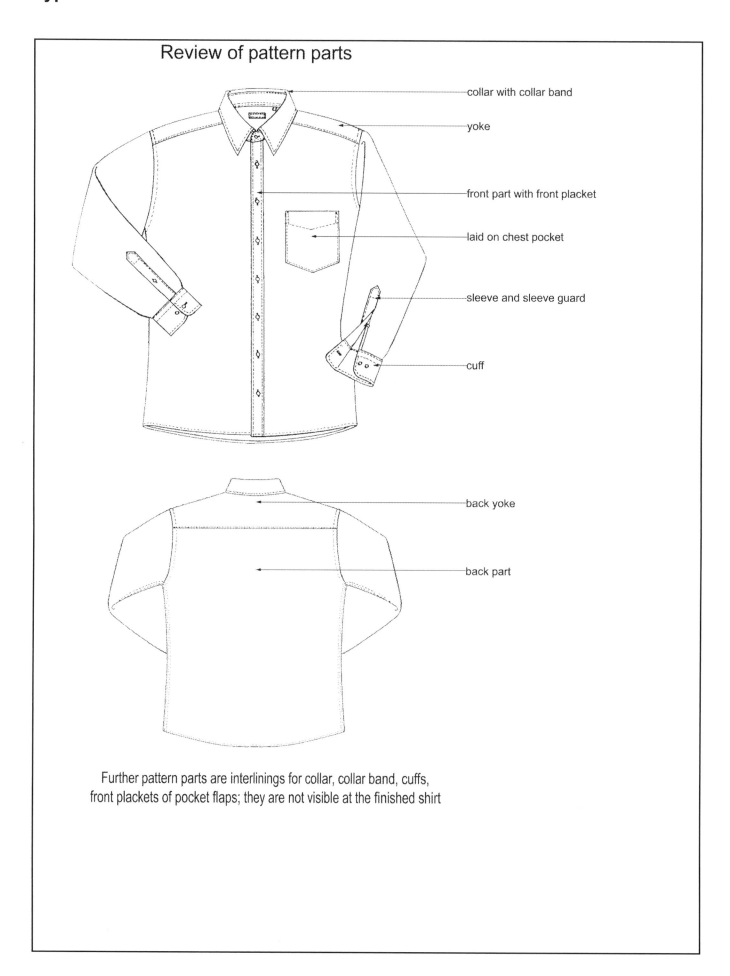

Review of pattern parts

collar with collar band

yoke

front part with front placket

laid on chest pocket

sleeve and sleeve guard

cuff

back yoke

back part

Further pattern parts are interlinings for collar, collar band, cuffs,
front plackets of pocket flaps; they are not visible at the finished shirt

Front parts and fastenings

Front parts and fastenings (plackets)

Synopsis

Men's shirts – as all garments for men – are closed from left (over wrap) to the right (under wrap). The fastening is – with exception of some casual shirts – vertical at centre front. To improve the optic and the quality in usage the front is folded in or a band of fabric is laid on, this forms the "front placket".

We differentiate between two kinds of fastenings – the open placket (the buttons are visible outside) and the covered placket, also called "covered fly front" (the buttons are covered by fabric and not visible outside). The covered placket is mainly used for formal or evening shirts. The following illustrations are standard practice front plackets in shirt manufacturing. Also the measurements in the form description next to the drawings are from experience and standards. They can be laid down in the appropriate measurement chart. Embroideries at the front or the usage of bigger buttons can require a wider front placket.

There are many other design alternatives apart from these standard front openings. But these come and go with current fashion trends, e.g.:

- Asymmetric or uniform fastenings
- John-Wayne-shirt
- Slip on-shirts or polo plackets (See also chapter "Design".)

Front parts and fastenings

Drawing

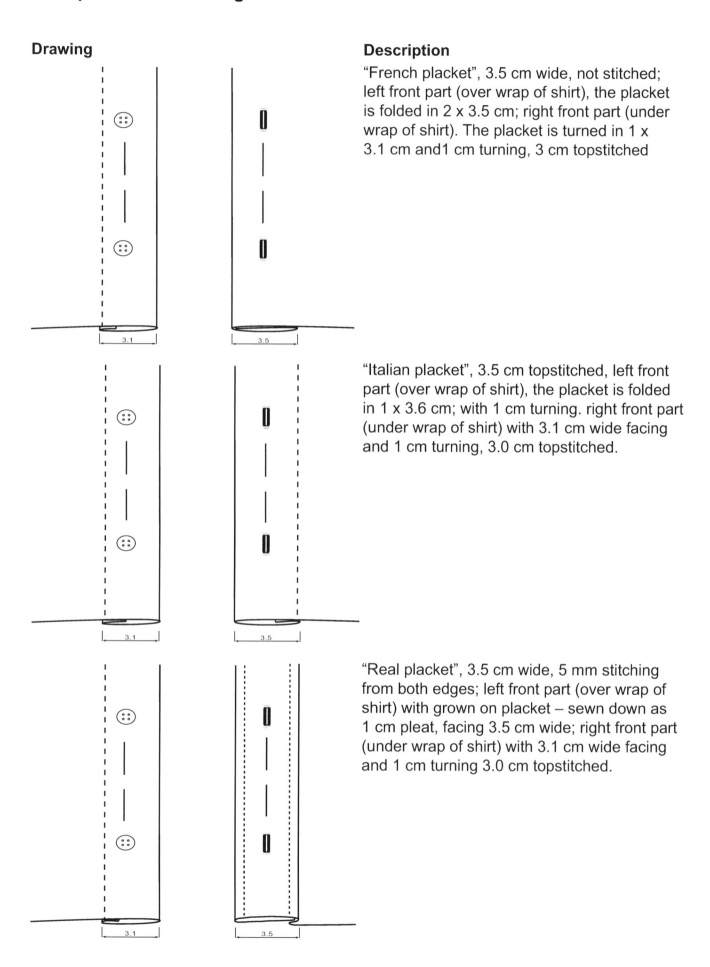

Description

"French placket", 3.5 cm wide, not stitched; left front part (over wrap of shirt), the placket is folded in 2 x 3.5 cm; right front part (under wrap of shirt). The placket is turned in 1 x 3.1 cm and1 cm turning, 3 cm topstitched

"Italian placket", 3.5 cm topstitched, left front part (over wrap of shirt), the placket is folded in 1 x 3.6 cm; with 1 cm turning. right front part (under wrap of shirt) with 3.1 cm wide facing and 1 cm turning, 3.0 cm topstitched.

"Real placket", 3.5 cm wide, 5 mm stitching from both edges; left front part (over wrap of shirt) with grown on placket – sewn down as 1 cm pleat, facing 3.5 cm wide; right front part (under wrap of shirt) with 3.1 cm wide facing and 1 cm turning 3.0 cm topstitched.

Front parts and fastenings

Drawing

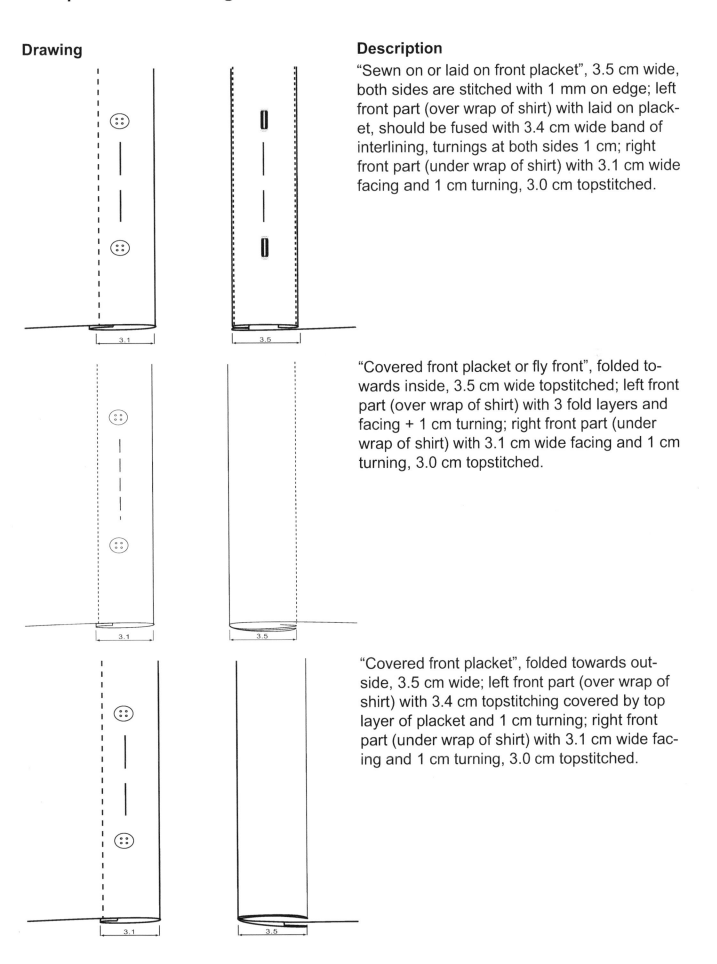

Description

"Sewn on or laid on front placket", 3.5 cm wide, both sides are stitched with 1 mm on edge; left front part (over wrap of shirt) with laid on placket, should be fused with 3.4 cm wide band of interlining, turnings at both sides 1 cm; right front part (under wrap of shirt) with 3.1 cm wide facing and 1 cm turning, 3.0 cm topstitched.

"Covered front placket or fly front", folded towards inside, 3.5 cm wide topstitched; left front part (over wrap of shirt) with 3 fold layers and facing + 1 cm turning; right front part (under wrap of shirt) with 3.1 cm wide facing and 1 cm turning, 3.0 cm topstitched.

"Covered front placket", folded towards outside, 3.5 cm wide; left front part (over wrap of shirt) with 3.4 cm topstitching covered by top layer of placket and 1 cm turning; right front part (under wrap of shirt) with 3.1 cm wide facing and 1 cm turning, 3.0 cm topstitched.

Front parts and fastenings

Measurement areas

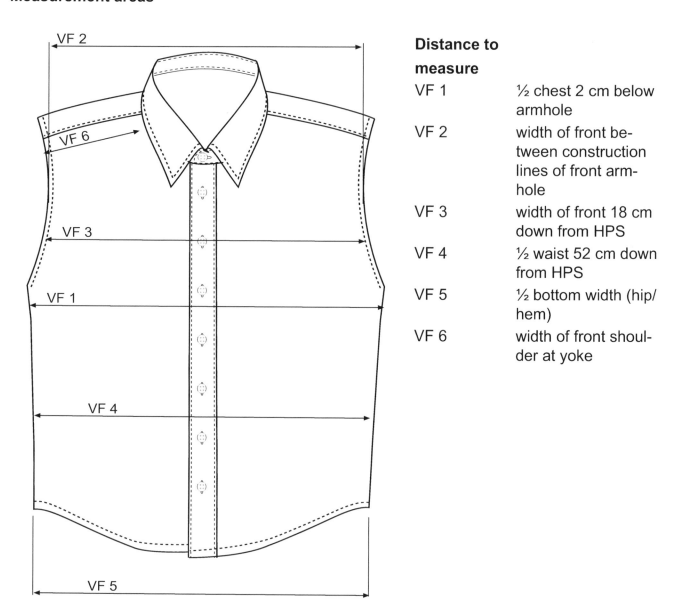

Distance to measure

VF 1	½ chest 2 cm below armhole
VF 2	width of front between construction lines of front armhole
VF 3	width of front 18 cm down from HPS
VF 4	½ waist 52 cm down from HPS
VF 5	½ bottom width (hip/ hem)
VF 6	width of front shoulder at yoke

Manufacturing advice

Plackets should be carefully pressed before sewing, to achieve a clean and even front. Plackets for formal shirts should be worked with interlining, to achieve a smooth and refined optic. The interlining can be fused or non fusible interfacing fixed through button holes and topstitching.

Special remark

The front of a shirt is an eye-catcher and especially noticed. Therefore it is most important to prepare and work the front plackets carefully and with the correct tension of the sewing machine to avoid puckering.

Back parts

Back parts

Synopsis

The most frequently used back parts are shown with the following illustrations (to get the complete pattern of the back part the drawing has to be doubled around the vertical centre back line)

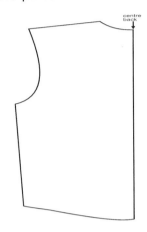

plain back part without yoke

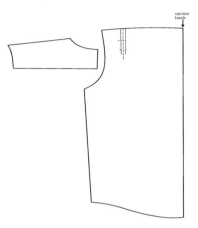

back part with 2 side pleats and yoke

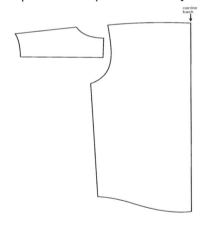

plain back part with yoke

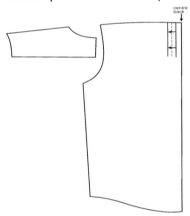

back part with box pleat at centre back and yoke

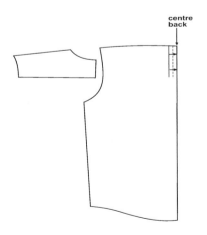

back part with inverted pleat at centre back and yoke

Back parts

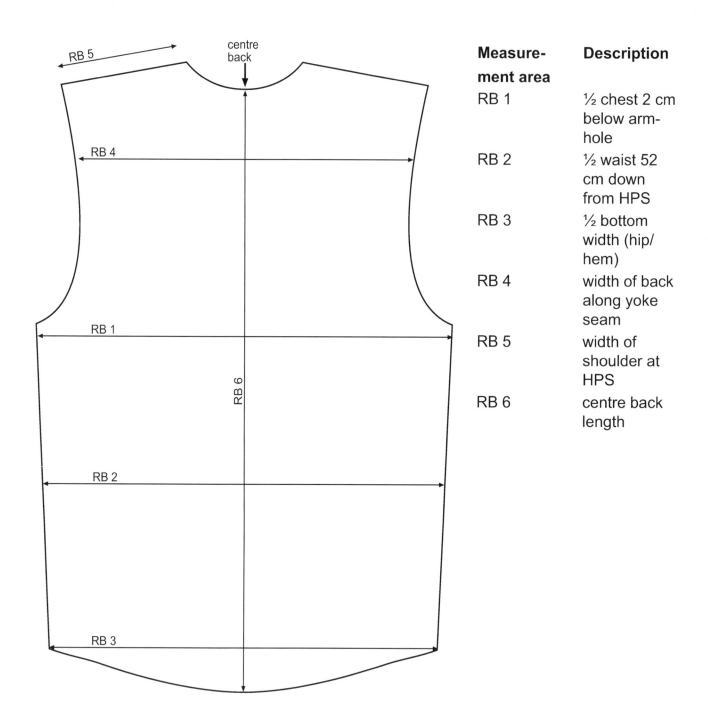

Measure-ment area	Description
RB 1	½ chest 2 cm below arm-hole
RB 2	½ waist 52 cm down from HPS
RB 3	½ bottom width (hip/hem)
RB 4	width of back along yoke seam
RB 5	width of shoulder at HPS
RB 6	centre back length

Manufacturing advice

If the back yoke is topstitched, lay outer yoke and the three seam allowances (outer yoke, inner yoke and back part) upwards and topstitch as per design or form description. The inner yoke folded downwards is not stitched. Both back yokes are then folded upwards and ironed into form and, if necessary, cut by that all edges are equal.

Sleeves

Sleeves

Synopsis
We differentiate between two kinds of sleeves for the standard men's shirt:
Long sleeve 1/1 length
Short sleeve 1/2 length
The short sleeve has a straight hemline with different form details at bottom of sleeve (See also pictures in chapter "Design".); the long sleeve finishes with a sleeve slit in a cuff.

Measurement areas:

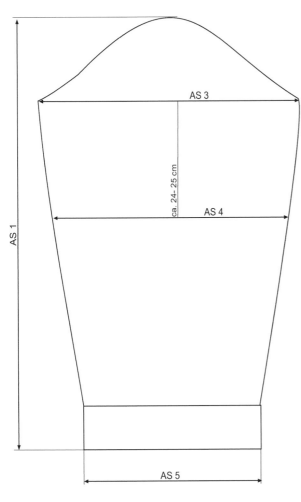
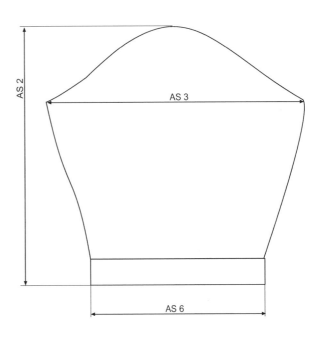

Code

AS1	long sleeve length from shoulder to bottom including cuff
AS 3	width of sleeve
AS 4	width of elbow, 24 to 25 cm from lower armhole
AS 5	bottom width of sleeve at cuff attachment seam

Code

AS 2	short sleeve length from shoulder to finished hem/bottom line
AS 3	width of sleeve
AS 6	sleeve opening at hem of short sleeve

Sleeves

All these measurements are part of the appropriate measurement chart.

Manufacturing advice

- ☞ Standard length for a long sleeve is approx. 63 – 65 cm from shoulder/armhole to bottom of sleeve including cuff.
- ☞ It is important to take also the total measurement of width of shoulder plus sleeve length. This measurement ranges from 82 to 84 cm. If the shoulder is prolonged (dropped) we have to shorten the sleeve accordingly to keep the total measurement (width of shoulder + sleeve length).
- ☞ Usually the sleeve length for a long sleeve is not graded but the same length is kept for all sizes. If the length is graded it should be in groups of sizes, e.g. sizes S, M, and L one length; sizes XL, XXL and XXXL 1 – 2 cm longer. Apart from standard sleeve lengths, shirts with extra long or extra short sleeves are offered. Usually these sleeves are approx. 5 cm longer or 5 cm shorter than the standard length. Extra long sleeves should also have a longer body (centre back length).

Certain forms of sleeves change with current fashion trends and then disappear for years.

Raglan sleeves   Dolman sleeves   Kimono sleeves

Collar

Collar

Synopsis
The collar is one of the most important elements of the shirt, beside material, colour, etc. The collar consists of several components, therefore at first a synopsis of the single parts.

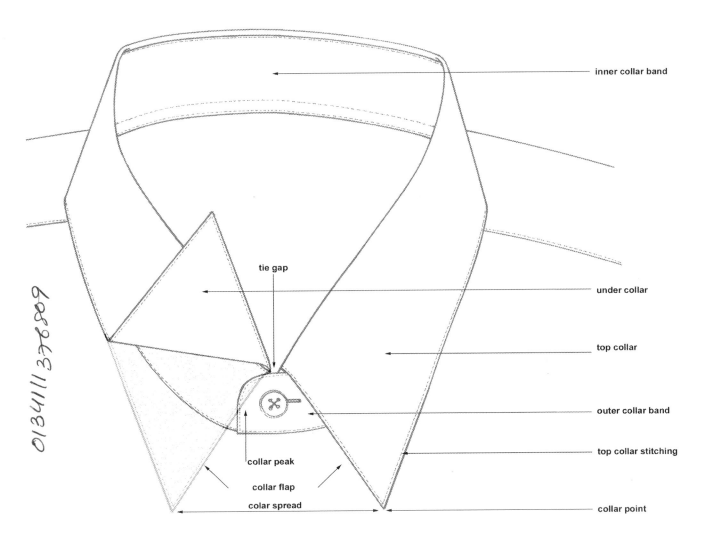

Generally we differentiate between

- ☞ One-piece collars: collar and collar band are cut and sewn in one piece.

- ☞ Two-piece collars: collar and collar band are cut separately and joined together after the collar is sewn.

- ☞ Special forms: e.g. stand-up collar, wing-collar, grown-on collar or knitted collar.

Predominant in shirt collections are two-piece collars. Their fit is exact and perfected and therefore used for formal and business shirts.
The shape and fit of one-piece collars is softer; these collars are more suitable for leisure-wear shirts, casual and informal models.

Collar

The most important collar forms, their names and description

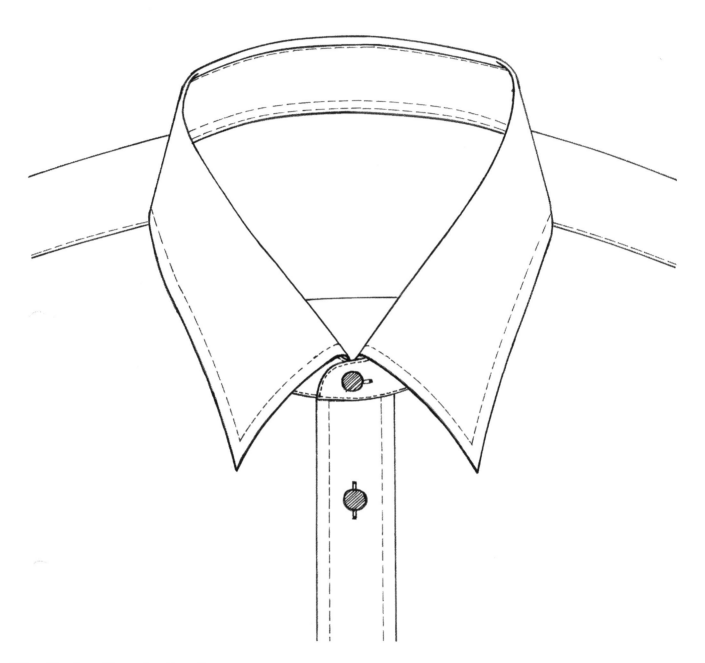

"Kent", also "London" collar

Generally this two-piece collar is the classic shirt collar! Length of collar flap is approx. 7.5 cm, collar spread approx. 11 – 12 cm, tie gap 0.3 – 0.5 cm. This classic collar is suitable for all formal shirts, but also for informal styles and has mostly two collar interlinings (basic collar interlining and collar patch on top); for very correct shapes soft collar bones (collar sticks) are inserted.

Collar

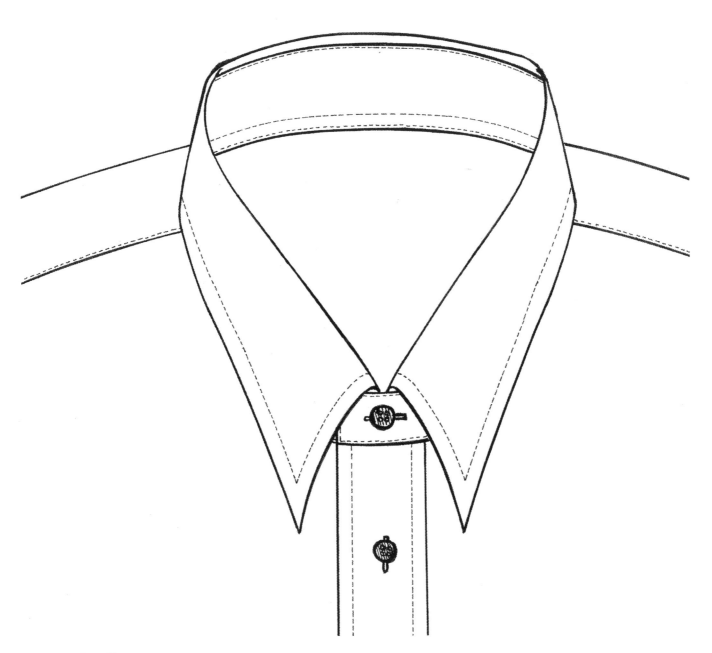

"Italian" collar

Like the "Kent" this collar is a 2-piece collar, but the shape is different. The collar flaps are longer (8.0 – 8.5 cm), the collar points stand closer and the collar spread is with approx. 8.0 – 9.0 cm smaller. The cut shows a slim and elegant, longer collar.

Collar

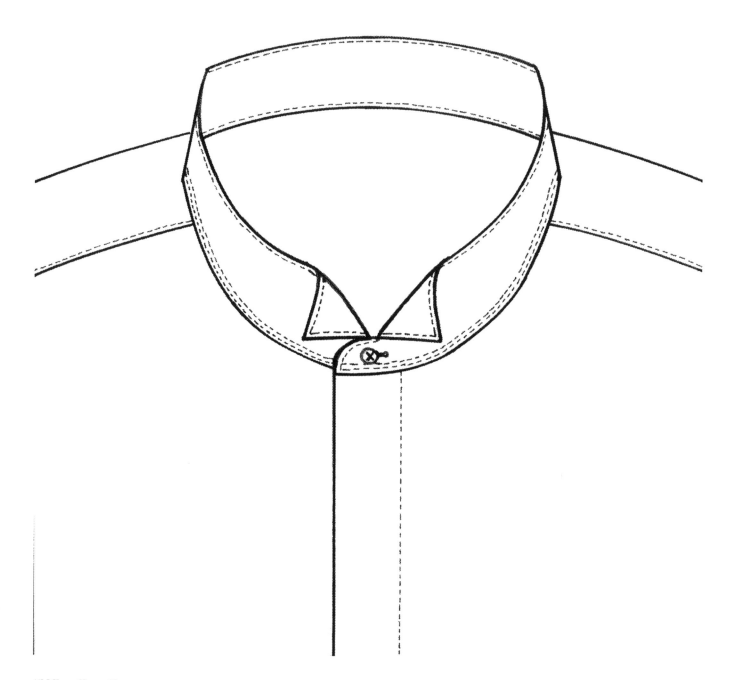

"Wing" collar

An especially formal stand-up collar with small wings or flaps as part of evening wear, mainly worn with black bow tie at festive occasions. This collar got a nick name in Germany "Vater - Mörder" (parricide) because it was stiff and sometimes uncomfortable. Shirts with wing collars have mostly covered front fastenings.

Collar

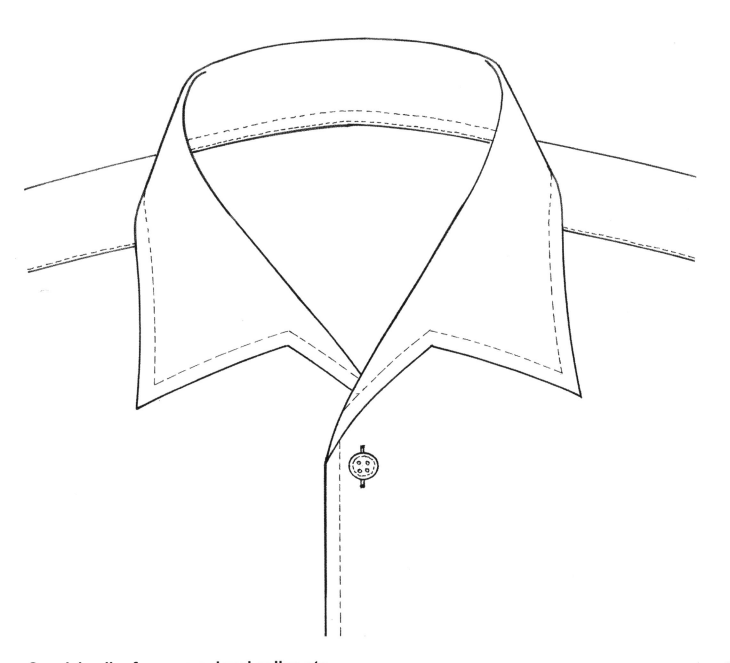

Special collar forms, e.g. lapel collar, etc.

This one-piece collar seems to be an extension of the front parts. As there are many ways of wearing possible, this collar is called "Vario" collar. (see also topic "Design details").

Collar

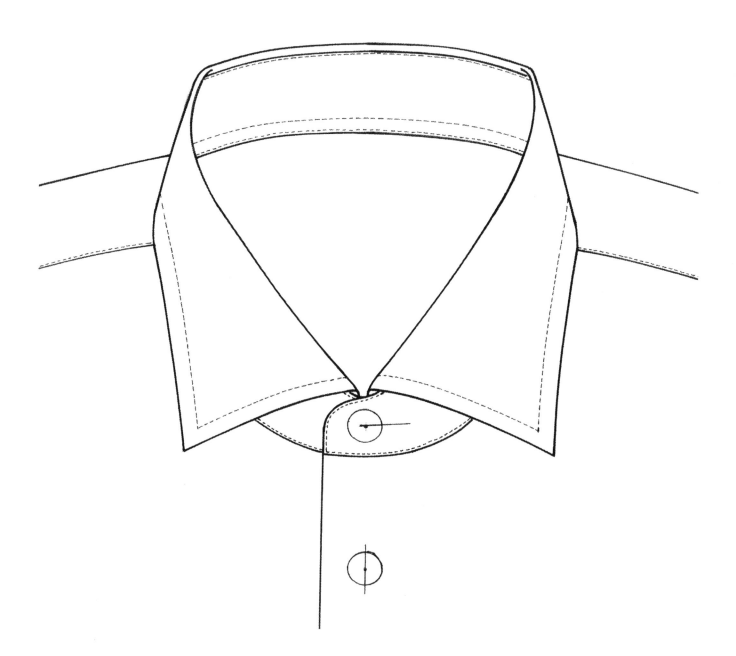

"Shark fin" collar

This collar form is extremely wide spread (up to 16 cm), the length of collar flaps is approx. 7.5 to 8.0 cm and the collar points are moved backwards. The tie gap can be up to 7 mm. This type of collar is especially suitable for formal shirts; because of the wide collar spread and bigger tie gap heavier ties with big knot can be worn. These cut away wider spread collars need collar bones or collar sticks.

Collar

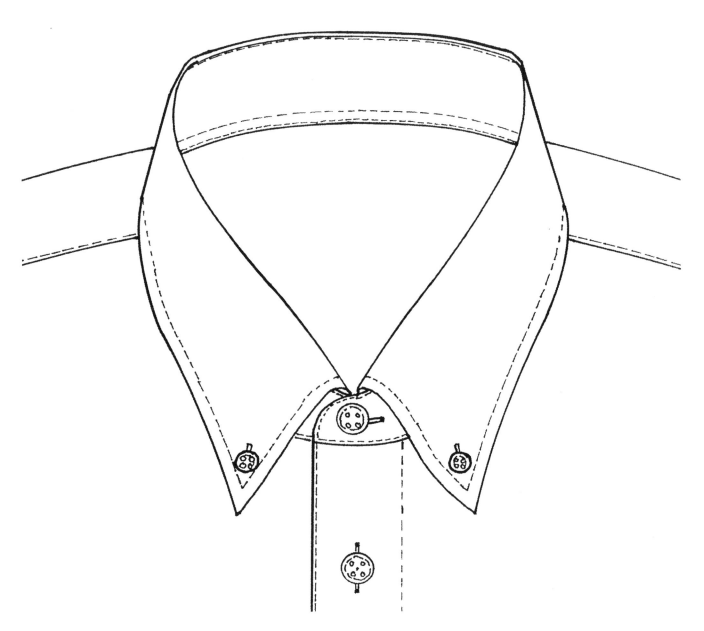

"Button-down" collar

It is an informal variation of the "Kent" collar. The collar points are buttoned down onto the front parts. This collar has only basic fusible interlining (no reinforcement interfacing and never collar bones). The buttons to fix the collar points are small, normally 14'" with exception 16'". The button position is strengthened (reinforced) through an under laid small piece of self fabric or non fusible interlining.

Collar

Collar topstitching

Before the usage of hot melt adhesive interlinings became popular, the interfacing material was fixed through topstitching of collar. There are a great number of stitching variations and they are an important element of design. Also topstitching in contrast yarns and colour or different types of stitches are possible.

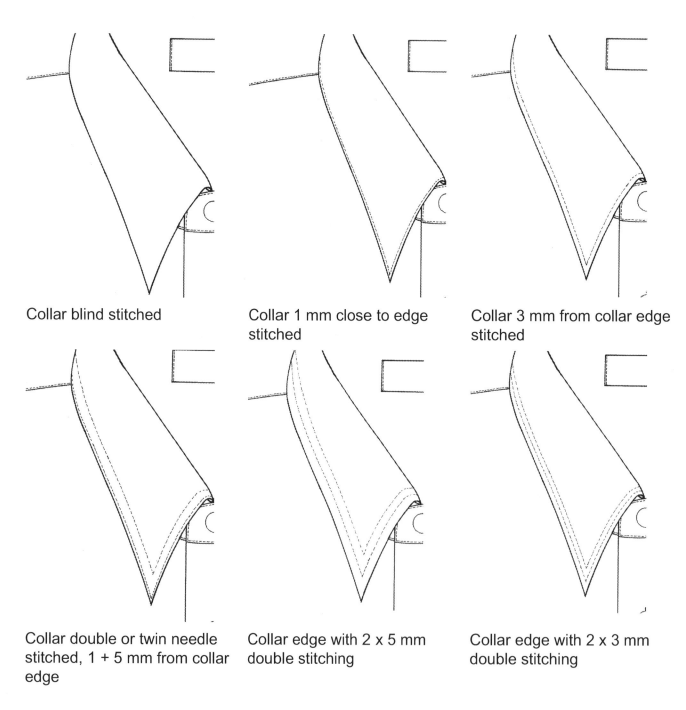

Collar blind stitched

Collar 1 mm close to edge stitched

Collar 3 mm from collar edge stitched

Collar double or twin needle stitched, 1 + 5 mm from collar edge

Collar edge with 2 x 5 mm double stitching

Collar edge with 2 x 3 mm double stitching

For further topstitching ideas see topic "Design details".

Collar

Measuring areas

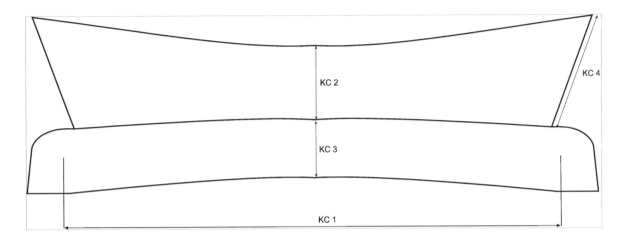

Measurement points	Distance to measure
KC 1	real width of collar in finished shirt, measure from centre front to centre front of collar band
KC 2	height of collar at centre back
KC3	height of collar band at centre back
KC4	length of collar flaps / collar points

For men's outer wear or ready-made garments, e.g. jackets, coats etc. the size refers to the chest measurement. But for shirt sizes the manufacturing industry takes the neck circumference or length of the collar. We use the neck measurement to construct the collar, but when we check the collar length measurement/size it is taken in the middle of the collar band from centre front to centre front, e.g. centre of button to 2 mm inside beginning of button hole. Therefore neck circumference and collar length differ a little.

Some clients want the average height of collar at centre back, which is calculated: Height of collar band CB (e.g. 3.5 cm) plus height of collar CB (e.g. 4.5cm) equals 8cm divided by 2 is average height of collar of 4 cm.

When we define the shirt sizes to develop a measurement chart, we have "single sizes" e.g. 39, 40, 41, 42, 43, 44, etc. or "double sizes" = M, L, XL, XXL. The single size 39 and 40 correspond with the double size M (see diagram below).

Single size	39/40	41/42	43/44	45/46	47/48
Double size	M	L	XL	XXL	XXXL

If we have size 41/42 = L in the measurement chart the body pattern has always the measurements of the bigger size, here 42.

Normally the length of the collar band is slightly longer than the measurement of size label. This differs from company to company and can be between 5 to 10 mm more, e.g. size 42, but the measured collar length is 42.5 cm. The collar can shrink a little during fusing of interlining or washing.

Collar

Manufacturing advice

- The under collar must not have too much fullness or length.
- The non fused outer collar band must not be distorted and should not have too much fullness.
- The sewn out collar edge must be correct without piping (under collar must not be visible on top).
- The collar topstitching must be even and without joins.
- The tie gap and collar spread (distance collar point to collar point) must be according to instruction or form analysis.

Cuffs

Cuffs

Synopsis

The cuff is the decorative and functional ending of a long sleeve. The 1/1 sleeve has 1 or 2 pleats, sleeve slit with sleeve placket or sleeve guard and is attached into the cuff with 1 cm seam allowance. The sleeve slit extends the sleeve opening and makes it easier to put on the shirt or even to roll up the sleeves. (See detailed descriptions of cuff and sleeve plackets in the following chapters.)
We differentiate between 5 basic forms of cuffs:

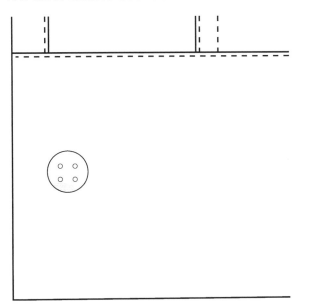

Cuffs with straight corners / rectangular cuffs

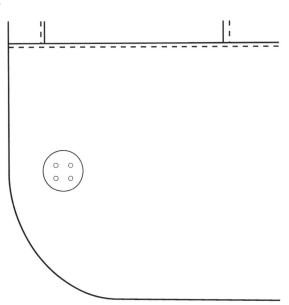

Cuffs with rounded corners / rounded cuffs

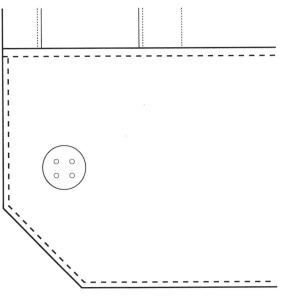

Cuffs with cut or "broken" corners / bevelled cuffs

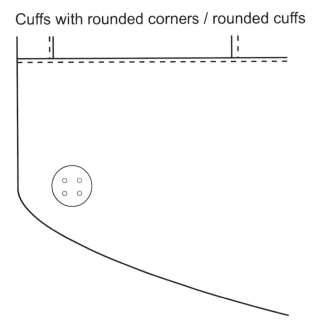

Cuffs with rounded corners / rounded cuffs curved cuff

Cuffs

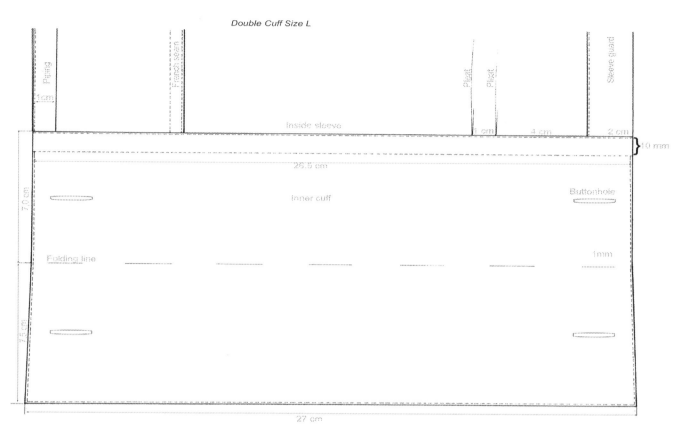

Double Cuff Size L

Turn up cuffs; the cuff is folded back in the middle of cuff. These double cuffs are worn with cuff–links and used for formal and elegant shirts.

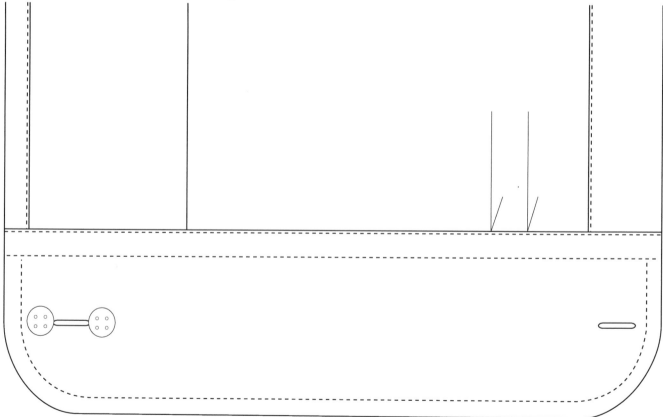

Combi cuff: The cuff can be closed with normal button or alternatively with cufflinks.
If the wearer decides to wear the shirt with cufflinks, the normal shirt buttons should be removed

Cuffs

Measuring areas

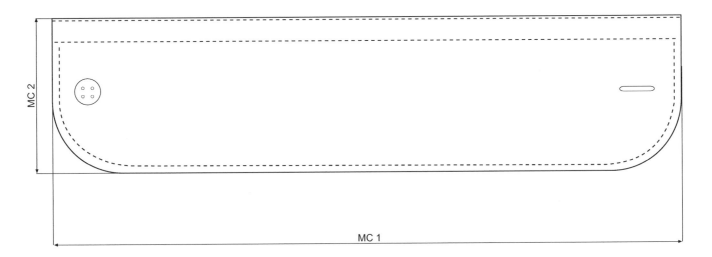

Code	Measurement
MC 1	Cuff length from edge to edge
MC 2	Width of cuff, also height of cuff

The standard height of cuff is approx. 6 to 7 cm with 1 x 16''' or 18''' button or 2 buttons parallel, to adjust the cuff opening (to make it smaller). The distance between the 2 buttons is 2.5 cm (centre of buttons). Fashion shirts with 2, 3 or more buttons are feasible; the width of cuff has to be bigger accordingly.

Many measurement charts give the cuff length as buttoned cuff (closed). This means: Cuff length from edge to edge e.g. 26.5 cm minus 1 cm (cuff edge to beginning of button hole) and minus 1.2 cm (cuff edge to centre of 1st button) = finished cuff length buttoned is approx. 24 to 24.3 cm.

Cuffs

Manufacturing advice

- Form, shape and topstitching of cuff, grading of cuff length, finished measurements, position and numbers of buttons / buttonholes is recorded in detail in the form description, processing instructions and/or technical detail drawings (scale 1 : 1).

- The outer cuff is fused with interlining. The interfacing can reach into the cuff seam (sewn out edge), but in most cases the interlining is cut in net measurements/shape of the finished cuff.

- Then the stitching of outer and inner cuff (sewing out) takes place at the edge of the interlining. The non fused inner cuff must not have too much fullness or length and should not be distorted. Cuffs must be cut as a pair (same form and pattern of fabric e.g. stripe or check) and should be worked together and not be separated during manufacturing.

- When the sleeves are attached into the cuffs, the sleeves must not be stretched or the pattern distorted (see illustrations below).

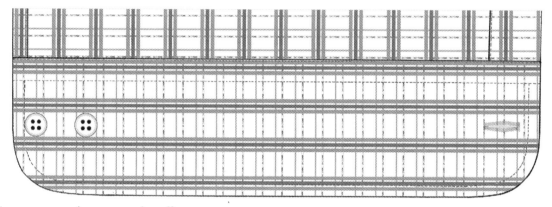

Correct sewn on sleeve and cuff

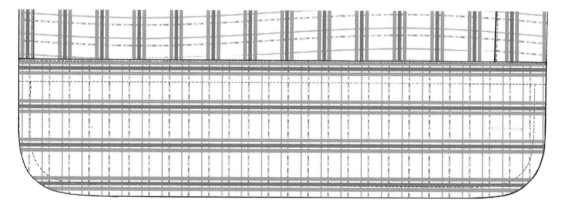

Bad workmanship, the fabric of the sleeve is distorted

Sleeve plackets (also sleeve guards)

Sleeve plackets (also sleeve guards)

Synopsis

For a standard man's shirt we differentiate between the following sleeve plackets:

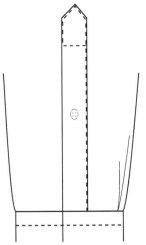

Classic roof placket, usually 15 – 16.5 cm long, with slit opening 12 -13 cm, width of placket is normally 2.5 max 3 cm.
Here the sleeve placket is buttoned.

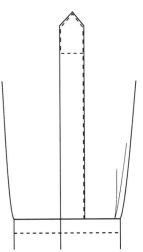

Classic roof placket, usually 15 – 16.5 cm long, with slit opening 12 -13 cm, width of placket is normally 2.5 max 3 cm.
Here the sleeve placket is not buttoned.

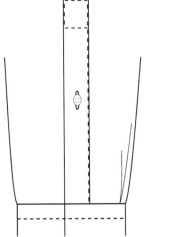

Square sleeve placket, buttoned with a small 14''' button and vertical buttonhole.

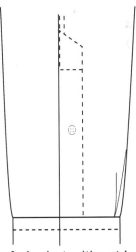

Asymmetrical roof placket without button, as continuation of a seam at the back of sleeve. Slit facings and under wrap are grown on.

The Name "roof placket" is given because the top of the placket is pointed and has a shape like the roof of a house. There are also straight or asymmetrical endings for sleeve plackets.

Sleeve plackets (also sleeve guards)

Measuring areas

These measurements are used as control measurements for production only; they do rarely occur in the measurement chart.

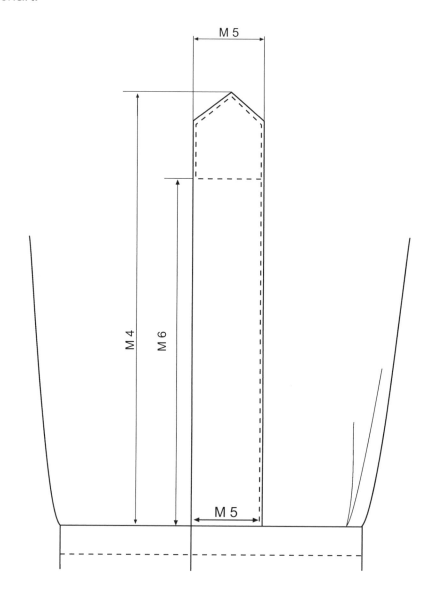

Code	Measurement
M 4	length of sleeve placket (roof placket)
M 5	Width of sleeve placket
M6	length of slit opening

Manufacturing advice

- ☞ Sleeve plackets can be distorted and slanting attached to the cuff or there can be puckering through bad sewing tension at the sleeve placket and/or sleeve.

Shoulder yokes

Synopsis

Having a shoulder yoke raises the comfort in wearing the shirt because there is no seam pressing down on the highest line of the shoulder; the front yoke is moved forward 4 – 5 cm, the back yoke lies backward 5 – 8 cm from the highest line of the shoulder (measured at armhole), depending on height of back yoke at centre back. The shoulder yoke underlines the shoulder area as the yokes are cut horizontal or sometimes diagonal / on bias.
Generally we differentiate between:

- Double back yokes and
- Single back yokes

For double back yokes there are two pieces of fabric, usually cut horizontal – the outer and the inner yoke. The face side of fabric is showing to the outside. All seam allowances of front parts; both yokes and back part lie between the two yokes and are not visible. The garment is clean from the inside. The main label and sometimes special labels e.g. "iron free" or "two ply" … are sewn onto the inner yoke (see topic label and label positions).

Single yokes consist of one piece of fabric, usually cut horizontal. If the main label is stitched onto the yoke at centre back, the sewing stitches are visible outside at the back. Inside the shirt the seam allowances are visible.
For shirts without shoulder yoke (back is cut in one piece) sometimes a rounded piece of fabric is used as back neck facing (so called "half moon"). It also carries the labels (see sketch next page). When you look inside the collar of the folded shirt, you get the impression of an inner yoke. (See sketches next page.)

Manufacturing advice

- To attach labels, embroidery or print logos on the inner back yoke is the first step in manufacturing process.

- When the back yoke is topstitched, e.g. 1 mm or 5 mm from the seam, the back yoke + the 3 seam allowances of back yoke, inner yoke and back part are laying towards one side and topstitched as per design or form description. The inner yoke lies to the opposite side and is not topstitched.

Shoulder yokes

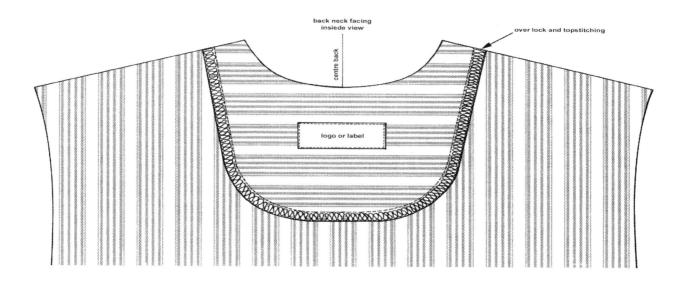

Here the half moon facing is cut horizontal in the stripe to create the impression of an inner yoke.

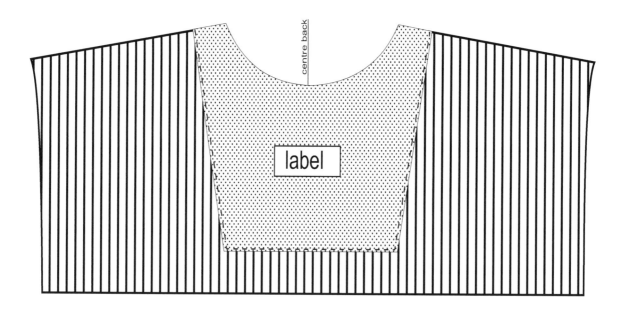

A variation is a back facing. Facing is of pique material laid on inside of back part. 1 cm turnings are folded in and the edge is topstitched 1 mm, a better and cleaner solution.

Shoulder yokes

Measuring areas

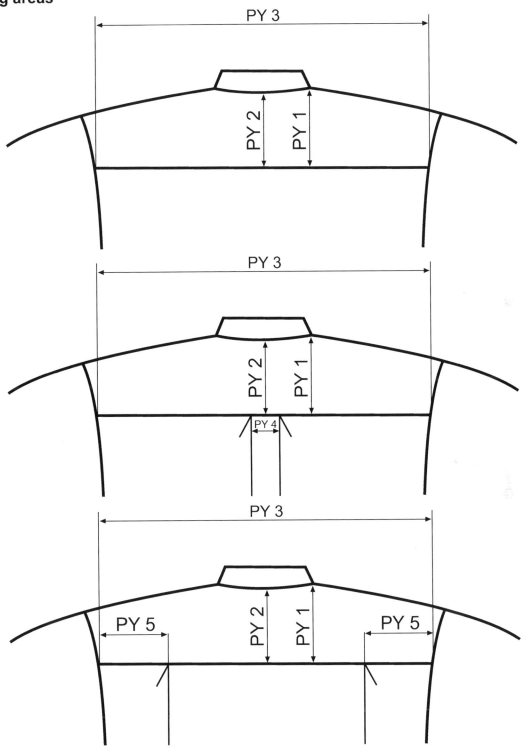

Code	Measurement
PY 1	height of back yoke at HPS
PY 2	height of back yoke at centre back
PY 3	width of back at yoke seam
PY 4	width of box pleat
PY 5	position of side pleats (distance from armhole, measured along the yoke seam), usually 9 cm from armhole and for XL sizes 11cm from armhole seam.

Pockets

Pockets

Synopsis

The mostly used pocket on a man's shirt is the laid on chest or patch pocket. We differentiate between 6 basic pockets forms

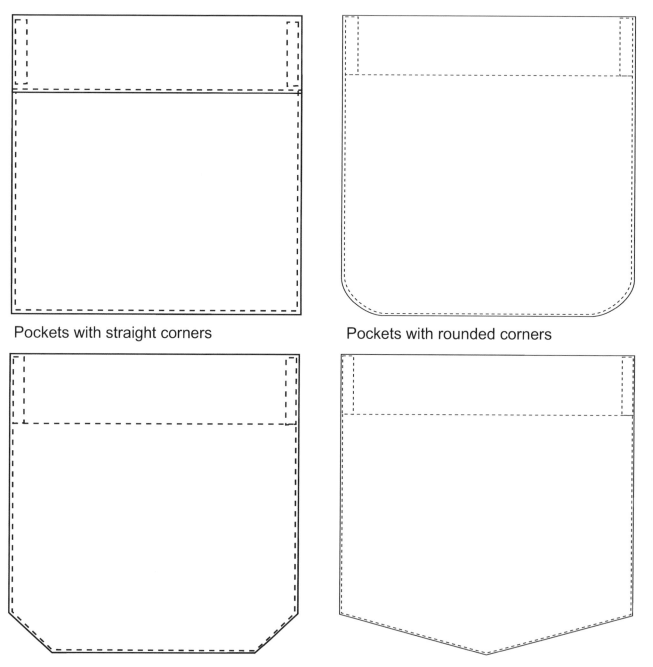

Pockets with straight corners

Pockets with rounded corners

Pockets with cut or "broken" corners / bevelled pockets

Pointed 5 corner pockets also V-shape pocket

Pockets

Special Forms are:

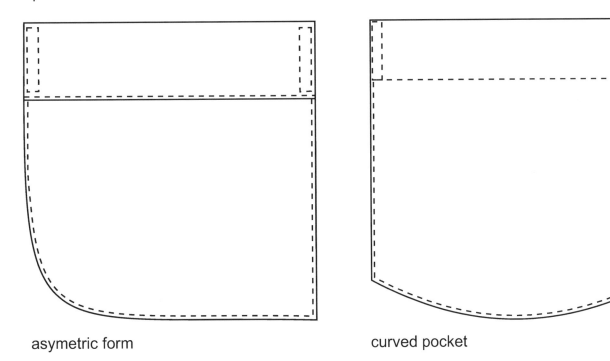

asymetric form   curved pocket

Manufacturing advice

The laid on chest pocket is used mostly as a single pocket on the left front part. The position is approximately 20 to 22cm below the shoulder seam and 6.5 cm from centre front of the shirt for sizes S- L. For bigger sizes the distance from centre front to the pocket must be graded. Special types of shirts, e.g. pilot shirts or uniform shirts, etc. can have pockets on both fronts. The position is analogue on both fronts.
The chest pocket can either be flat and stitched on with 1mm as a patch on the front part or, can have a pleat to increase the volume of the pocket.
The pocket opening should be locked with a backstitch or bar tuck on both sides to secure the pocket usage. The pocket facing can be straight and just folded in or pointed and stitched down.

Most pockets are not buttoned. If buttoning is requested, the position of button and the direction of the buttonhole must be illustrated in a production sketch.

Pockets

Measuring areas

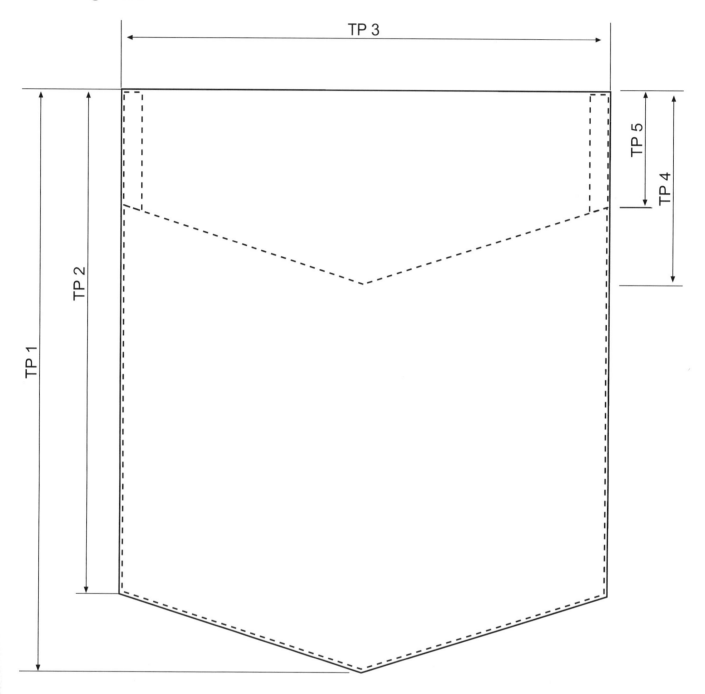

Code	Measurement
TP 1	Total length of pocket
TP 2	Length of pocket on short side
TP 3	Width of pocket
TP 4	Depth point of V-shape facing
TP 5	Facing at sides of chest pocket

Pockets

Pocket flaps

If pockets are closed with a pocket flap and buttoned, the direction of the buttonhole is usually vertical. The button is fastened securely on the pocket underneath. Also the application of press buttons, snap fastener or velcro tape is possible to close the pocket flap.
The pocket flap is cut approx. 4 mm wider than the width of the pocket to cover 2mm on both sides. In form the flap follows the shape of the pocket, e.g. here both with cut corners. A pocket flap protects the content of the pocket and prevents it from falling out. This is the reason, why most uniform and service shirts have pockets with flaps.

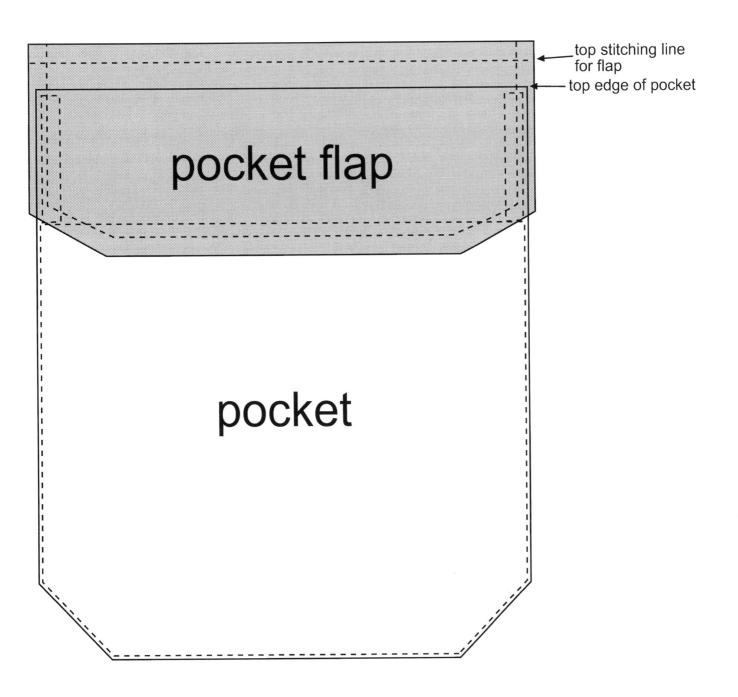

top stitching line for flap
top edge of pocket
pocket flap
pocket

Fibres

Synopsis

The fabric plays a central role in the quality and price of the shirt. It determines appearance, effect, comfort of wear and durability. Equally decisive are raw material and fibres (Composition of fabric). There are many publications about fibres therefore this book mentions only the most important.
Fibres are classified into two main groups:

- Natural fibres and
- Chemical fibres

Summary of fibres

Cotton
For shirts the mostly used fibre is cotton. Cotton is pleasant on the skin. It absorbs sweat well. It is inexpensive and it provides excellent care qualities. Slightly negative points are: Cotton tends to shrink and is crease susceptible. There are a number of chemical and mechanical procedures to improve shrinkage and creasing e.g. mercerize, calender or sanforize cotton. Cotton is often mixed with chemical fibres e.g. Polyester. Pure (100%) Cotton is used for all types of shirts and it is still the No. 1 shirt fabric. Two cotton-mix materials are also popular:
CVC = Portion of cotton is higher than chemical fibres.
TC = There are more chemical fibres than cotton.

Linen
Linen is often used for casual and traditional/country-style shirts. The fibre is harder and thicker than cotton. The feel and texture of linen material is rustic and more robust. The cooling effect makes linen to a popular fibre for summer garments.
Pure linen tends to crease extremely and this might be the main reason why 100% linen is never used for formal shirts. Because production of pure linen cloth is complicated and expensive, linen in weft is combined with cotton in warp. The fabric is smoother and it is named "Half Linen".

Wool
Pure wool is insignificant for shirt manufacturing and very rarely used. There are special brands using cotton/wool-mix fabrics (55/45) e.g. "Viyella" for casual shirts, sometimes brushed (flannel) and with check patterns (tartans). It is here very important to follow the washing instructions.

Silk
Silk is the most luxurious fabric for shirts. Formal and evening shirts get this special "noble" look with silk. Some years ago silk was used for printed casual shirts (1980s).
Silk feels pleasantly cool in hot temperature. Silk shirts should be washed with special care. It is the most delicate fibre.

Fibres

Chemical fibres

Synopsis

The great advantage of chemical fibres is that these fibres can be produced in nearly unlimited quantity and in one constant high quality and for a price, which is a fraction for natural fibres. Today chemical fibres can be "designed" to imitate the grip and look of natural fibres, or they hat attributes attributes, which are not inherent in natural fibres. (e.g. non flammable technical fabrics.) Nevertheless chemical fibres did not achieve strong position in shirt fashion. A good example is the „Nyltest" shirt of the 60ies. In combination with cotton these fabrics are still popular and accepted because of their easy-care attributes.
We distinguish between two main groups:

Cellulose based fibres

Cellulose is the raw material. After different procedures the thread can be spun. The best known fibres are acetate copra and viscose.

Pure synthetics

The source is mineral oil which is the base material for all manmade fibres. There are three main groups of synthetics:

- Polyamide (Nyltest is a fibre of polyamide.)
- Polyacryl
- Polyester

All fibres have different attributes in use and care.

Mixed fibres

To improve the attributes and quality of a fabric, natural fibres are mixed with chemical fibres. In the shirt production two combinations are very successful:

- CVC Portion of cotton is higher than chemical fibre.
- TC Portion of cotton is less than chemical fibres

Fabrics and fibres

Woven and knitted fabrics

Synopsis

Fabrics obtain characteristic patterns and features through cross-weaving and density of warp and weft threads (textile technology).

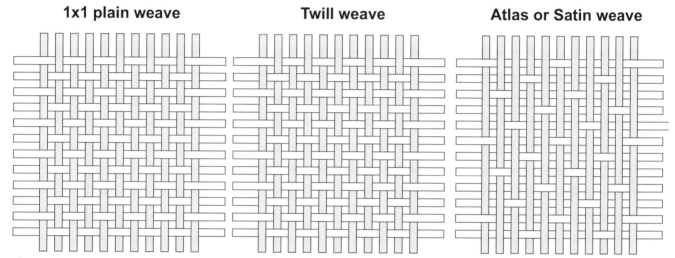

1x1 plain weave	Twill weave	Atlas or Satin weave
One warp and one weft thread is crossing in turns.	Used for flannels, twills, gabardines – The most common construction is 2x1 weave. This weaving-pattern creates a diagonal line in shirting. This appearance is particularly noticeable in gabardines due to special construction.	Used for satins, jacquard weaving, damask, brocade, matelassé and satin découpé. The binding/weaving points are in an irregular pattern. This causes a smooth and shiny surface; often used for shirting with satin-stripes on the surface of the fabric, also called "dobby weave".

Special weave

Corduroy and Velvet

Knitted and automatic knitted fabrics

We differ between knitted fabrics (the knitting needle is fixed) and automatic knitted materials (the knitting needle is moved during manufacturing process). The mesh picture/structure is the same. Knitted fabrics used for shirts are piqué, jersey and interlock.

Fabrics and fibres

Here are some fundamental terms in textile shirting technology

Flannel
Flannel fabric is brushed either on one or both sides of the material. The brushing can be "heavy brushed" or "light brushed". Brushing is being done during the finishing process.

Gingham
Light yarn dyed fabrics in 1x1 weave with 26 warp threads to 24 weft threads per square cm.

Lawn
Lightweight shirting in 1x1 weave, using fine and high quality yarns.

Poplin
Common name for shirt fabrics in 1x1 weave, which have more warp than weft threads (ideally nearly double count of warp over weft threads).
Simple poplin – made in normal non-twisted yarns
Half twist poplin – the warp using twisted yarn, for weft normal yarn
Full twist poplin – warp and weft using twisted yarns

Blended fabrics
In most cases of blended fabrics the yarns are already blends e.g. cotton mixed with polyester fibres. The idea is to use characteristics and advantages of certain fibres in a blended fabric for special purposes.

Indanthrene dyed
Original "vat dyes" with particularly high resistance to light, washing and bleaching.

Interlining (also interfacing)
These are especially finished fabrics (fusible or non-fusible) for re- inforcing collars, cuffs, front plackets, flaps etc. (see special chapter on "interlinings").

Non-iron
Fabrics are treated with chemicals in such a way that the shirt must not be ironed or is at least "easy-care" after washing in a washing machine.

Pre-shrunk fabrics
These are fabrics which are special treated and have shrinkage below 3%.

Resistance
Very loosely-woven materials often offer too little resistance to "wear and tear" and tend to pull away at the seams = "poor resistance".

Yarn thickness
In Germany yarn thickness is measured by NM = number metric e.g. NM 80 means 80 meters of a particular yarn weigh 1 gram; the higher the number the finer is the yarn.

Fabrics and fibres

Fabric requirements for men's shirts

- The fabric selection depends on use of the garment, e.g. is it a business, casual or working shirt? The most important criteria are pattern and colour of material, composition, design of garment and comfort of wear.
- The fabric must possess all quality aspects in fabrication and finishing as assured by the fabric supplier. Weaving faults, dirt or stains, foreign fibres and other irregularities, like colour shading or distortion, are not acceptable. Shrinkage must not exceed the specification guaranteed by the fabric supplier.
- Colour fastness must be guaranteed.
- Shrinkage, colour fastness and fabric reaction can be found out through washing and lab tests; these should be carried out during sampling process.
- Shirts are usually worn for hours directly on the skin and have to be washed very often, therefore the fabric should be washable and abrasion resistant. Also these tests should be done during sampling process.
- The fabric must warrant compatibility with environment and skin (health) of the wearer, e.g. the use of AZO colours or chrome VI colours is strictly forbidden.

Interlinings for shirts

Interlinings for shirts
Synopsis
Interlining is required in certain parts of the shirt e.g. collar, cuffs, front placket and special parts like shoulder flaps/epaulettes, tabs or pocket flaps etc. for form stability and to give the fabric a special smoothness. We distinguish between fusible interlinings with point coating and non-fusible interlinings without coating. Most shirt interlinings are in woven 100% cotton cloth, but there are also interlinings in fleece and new developments in stretch polyester woven fabric.
Leading manufacturers of shirt interlinings offer "temporary fused interlinings" for garment dyed and garment washed shirts. These interlinings have a particularly developed "temporary coating" which dissolves completely during the washing process of the manufactured shirt.
The desired handle of shirt parts with interlining, like softness and textile volume, is achieved through the correct choice and/or the right combination of interlinings. In 2006/07 the trend towards volume and soft handle persists and a contrary trend towards "flat collars and cuffs" is not yet visible. To obtain this handle mainly brushed interlinings are recommended.

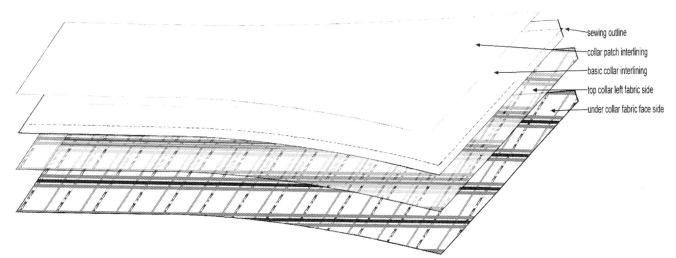

For classic and formal collars e.g. Kent, New Kent and Shark fin two types of collar interlinings are used. First there is the basic interlining on the top collar and additional a patch interlining. The basic interlining is approx. 5mm bigger than collar seam. The patch is 1-2 mm smaller than the collar seam and 5 mm less at collar break so collar rolls better.

Weights of shirt interlinings
Interlinings come from approximately 50 g/ m^2 up to approx. 285 g/ m^2.
Fusing conditions of interlinings
The correct fusing of interlinings depends on three processing data:
- ☞ Temperature (Glue line)
- ☞ Pressure
- ☞ Fusing time

Recommended conditions

Weight of interlining	50 – 105 gr./m²	110 - 285 gr./m²
Temperature	160-165°C	165-175°C
Pressure	15- 25N/cm² or 2 -3 bar	15- 25N/cm² or 2 -4 bar
Fusing time	12 – 18 sec.	12 – 18 sec.

Interlinings for shirts

It is strongly recommended to follow the processing and technical advice of the interlining supplier, but to do fusing and washing tests additionally before starting bulk production. In case of manufacturing problems the interlining supplier will help and assist you with a highly qualified technical service and excellent laboratory.

Combinations of shirt interlinings
The combination of interlining depends on the type of shirt, how stiff and formal or soft and casual the shirt should look. (For Type of shirt, see Chapter "Types of shirts".)

Formal tailored shirt
The collar shape is mostly a Kent-collar wider spread, or "New Kent" and "Shark fin". These collars have always collar-bones (fish-bones also collar-stays), either sewn-in or with a pocket for removable collar stays. The look is voluminous, collar and cuff edges are often wider topstitched e.g. 7 mm. Through the correct interlining combination we get a better textile hand-feel and the topstitching sinks more into the fabric – imitating a hand-tailored appearance with a bulky edge on collar and cuff.

Formal tailored and business shirt

Basic collar interlining	Approx. 230 gr./m^2
Collar patch interlining	Approx. 80 gr./ m^2
Collar band interlining	Approx. 230 gr./ m^2
Cuff interlining	Approx. 230 gr./ m^2
Front placket interlining	Approx. 80 gr./ m^2

Formal business shirt
Classic Kent- and New Kent-collars with a reduced curve on the outer collar edge still dominate the series of "Formal" shirts. For 2007 collections the cut-away New Kent-collar remains significant. The collar height at centre back has been reduced to 38 mm up to 42 mm. (Collar height = collar at centre back + collar band at centre back e.g. 4,5 cm + 3,5 cm = 8,0 cm divided by 2 = collar height of 40 mm).
For higher form stability, it is recommended to use a slightly stiffer interlining for the collar band. These collars have always collar bones.

Basic collar interlining	Approx. 170 gr./m^2
Collar patch interlining	Approx. 145 gr./ m^2
Collar band interlining	Approx. 170gr./ m^2
Cuff interlining	Approx. 170gr./ m^2
Front placket interlining	Approx. 80gr./ m^2

City dress shirt
The dominant Kent-collars and cuffs (rounded or with cut/broken corners) are noticeably softer than those of the Formal combination. To get this special textile hand-feeling, a middle weight basic collar interlining with a lighter collar patch interlining, both brushed, is recommended.

Basic collar interlining	Approx. 145 gr./m^2
Collar patch interlining	Approx. 80 gr./ m^2
Collar band interlining	Approx. 145 gr./ m^2
Cuff interlining	Approx. 145 gr./ m^2
Front placket interlining	Approx. 80 gr./ m^2

Interlinings for shirts

Semi-dress shirt

The collars are mainly classic Kent-collars or Italian Kent-collars with longer collar points and narrower collar spread. A softer and lighter basic collar interlining with approx. 100 g/m2 makes the collar not so stiff, but a light-weight collar patch still defines the collar break line precisely and gives the top collar a clean and even fall. Form stability is assured by using sewn-in, soft collar bones

Basic collar interlining	Approx. 100 gr./m^2
Collar patch interlining	Approx. 80 gr./ m^2
Collar band interlining	Approx. 100 gr./ m^2
Cuff interlining	Approx. 100 gr./ m^2
Front placket interlining	Mostly no front placket interlining

Casual shirt

Casual shirts have various collar forms – Kent-collar, Button-down-collar, variations of under-button-down-collars (also hidden-button-down), tab-collar, Piccadilly- collar. These special collars are particularly soft and self-supporting through their form and construction e.g. small 14''' buttons to fasten the collar flap onto the front part, or kept in shape through a tab or metal-pin. These collars are often seen with longer and more curved shanks (collar flaps), but never with collar bones!
If a Kent-collar for casual shirts should be a bit more formal, it is recommended to use a slightly heavier basic interlining but without a collar patch or with a extremely soft interlining as patch. This also applies for flannel shirts .

Basic collar interlining	Approx. 100 gr./m^2 or alternative lighter 80 gr./m^2
Collar band interlining	Approx. 100 gr./m^2 or alternative lighter 80 gr./m^2
Cuff interlining	Approx. 100 gr./m^2 or alternative lighter 80 gr./m^2
Front placket interlining	No front placket interlining

Fancy shirt

For this range a very soft interlining (80 gr./m^2) or an extremely soft and light- weight interlining without a collar patch is appropriate.
For genuine denim and garment washed shirts the best interlining weight is approx.
80 gr./m^2. This weight and the correct interlining quality is more suitable to counterbalance a possible higher shrinkage between top fabric and interlining during washing process than a light-weight interlining with micro point coating.

Basic collar interlining	Approx. 80 gr./m^2 or alternative lighter 50 gr./m^2
Collar band interlining	Approx. 80 gr./m^2 or alternative lighter 50 gr./m^2
Cuff interlining	Approx. 80 gr./m^2 or alternative lighter 50 gr./m^2
Front placket interlining	No front placket interlining

New Interlinings in stretch polyester woven fabric give a particularly subtle but also bulky effect.

Interlinings for shirts

Crash and Washer Shirts:

For shirts in materials with texture e.g. Crinkle, Seersucker etc. collars, cuffs, front plackets or other parts should not be fused, to keep the original character of the fabric. Non-fusible, sew-in interlining is the right choice. Also casual shirts that are "garment dyed" or "garment washed with enzymes" will get a soft, earthy effect and slightly "used look" after washing.

Basic collar interlining	Approx. 145 gr./m^2
Collar band interlining	Approx. 145 gr./m^2
Cuff interlining	Approx. 145 gr./m^2
Front placket interlining	No front placket interlining

New developments of temporary fused interlinings have a particularly developed "temporary" coating which is removed completely during washing process.

Pre-Cut interlining parts and tapes of interlining

For the shirt bulk production interlining for collar, cuffs, front placket and smaller parts, which have to be fused e.g. pocket flaps or tabs, is ordered by the yard or metre on a roll of approx. 100 metres. Then the factory has to cut the parts according to patterns. The problem occurs that the cut is not so precise especially the curve of collar nose or rounded cuffs, or length of collar flaps. As early as 1990, interlining suppliers have developed special computerised die cutting machines, which do the cutting of interlining more accurately. After providing patterns or popular collar shapes from the catalogue of the supplier, the required shirt interlinings are pre-cut (module punched) in form and size as per production order. Tapes for front plackets and seam stabilizing strips are cut in any required width on a roll.

Special manufacturing advice

- The interlining must be placed and ironed on in exact position and then fused under a fusing press, following the recommendations of the interlining supplier.
- It is advisable to make tests before starting bulk production.
- The temperature of the fusing press has to be checked from time to time as it can vary.
- The shrinkage of interlining is minimal – the washing shrinkage is ca. 0,5 -1% and the heating shrinkage approx. 0-0,3%. Manufacturers of interlinings advise that the top-fabric should not have shrinkage of more than 2% to avoid bubbling.
- The colour of the interlining should complement the fabric colour to avoid colour shading after fusing.
- Freshly fused parts should not be moved or handled while the coating is still warm and active, because there is a risk of getting marks.

Seams

Seams

Synopsis

In production we distinguish between:

- Closing seams with single-needle stitching
- Felled or lap-seams
- Safety and overlock seams
- Decorative topstitching

Single parts of the shirt are joined together with **closing seams**; the edges of seam allowances must be overlocked after the sewing process or the seam allowances are turned inside between 2 layers of fabric e.g. front shoulder seam or back yoke seam, but then without overlock stitch. The width of seam allowances is usually 10 mm.

With **felled** or **lap-seams** (also called "**French seams**") single parts of the garment are sewn together by turning in the seam-allowances; so that the inside and outside of the shirt is equally clean. A single or double row of stitches is visible on the outside, depending on type of seam. The width of seam-allowances is 10 to 14 mm.

Safety seams are mostly sewn on a "Rimoldi" machine. In one working process the seam is closed and the edges of the seam allowances are overlocked (overstitched). Surplus material is cut away by a knife in the sewing machine. The width of seam allowances is 8 to 10 mm depending on machine type (this must be checked with the requirements of the factory).

The optic of collars, cuffs, front edges, pockets etc. can be accentuated through decorative topstitching. There are many options and presentations possible. (See also chapter "topstitching on collar edge")

Seams

Description of seams and types of stitches

During the manufacturing process various kinds of seams are used, because there are different demands for durability on seams in certain parts of the shirt.

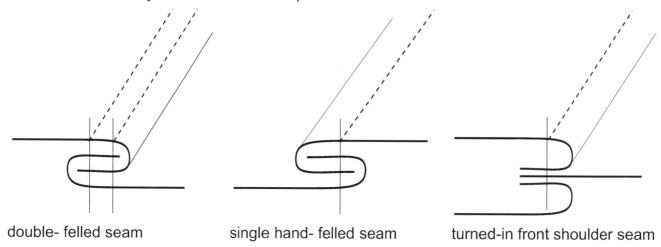

double- felled seam   single hand- felled seam   turned-in front shoulder seam

Types of stitches
In shirt manufacturing the following types of machine-stitch are predominantly used. (Definition follows ISO 4915):

Double lockstitch (301)

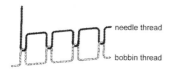

Used for all seams without strain

Double chain stitch (401)

for heavily used seams with special stress e.g. armholes

Three - thread over edge stitch (504)

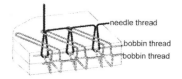

Two fabric parts are sewn together; edges of seam-allowances are overlocked together during the same process.

Seams

The **Double Lock stitch** type 301 is the mostly used stitch. It has a regular look on both sides of the fabric. This stitch type is susceptible to pucker. The reason is that the balance between the needle thread and bobbin is incorrect or the thread tension is too high. Unfortunately this stitch type is not very flexible on heavy used seams.

With the **Double Chain stitch** type 401 the needle thread forms pointed loops on the underside of the fabric; the bobbin thread gets pulled when unpicking the seam. The look is different between upper and under side of the fabric. For this stitch more yarn is needed because the bobbin thread needs the double distance to grip the needle thread; and the needle thread has to pick up the whole fabric. The advantage is that this stitch type is more flexible for harder used seams. Next to more yarn consumption also special sewing machines are needed.

With the **3-thread over-edge** (Safety) -stitch type 504 the fabric parts are sewn together and the edges are overlocked in the same process. Surplus fabric is cut away by a knife in the sewing machine; the overlocked edges should be clean. Though the 5-thread Safety-stitch has the highest yarn consumption, it is mainly used for lower priced shirts because the manufacturing process is very quick and the danger of puckering is relatively low. Even if the cutting was not so precise, the knife will smooth out the seams. A disadvantage of shirts with Safety-seams is that they do not look of "high-class" quality like shirts with felled seams.

The actual sewing process is a complicated combination of fabric reaction, tension of sewing machine for upper sewing-thread and bobbin, thickness of sewing-yarn and machine needle, transport of material in sewing process and handling the product by the machinist. It is most important that seams and topstitching are pucker free and workers do not attempt to correct bad sewing through "nice ironing". Puckering and bad workmanship will be visible after the first washing of the garment.

The most important points in sewing process are:

- Pressure on the machine presser
- Stitch type
- Machine needle
- Speed of sewing
- Stitch density
- Handling of sewing material

All these points have to be taken into consideration for the fabric and especially for "iron-free and easy-care" qualities.

Seams

Manufacturing advice

- In principle manufacturing must follow the given production instructions and form analysis. Any change of manufacturing process has to be confirmed by the client or with preceding permission of the client's technician while he visits the production factory. Fundamentally sewing and washing tests have to be done before starting bulk production with new fabrics or the repeat of previous production orders. The results of these tests have to be confirmed by the client to avoid problems with puckering, fabric reaction or shrinkage.
- The beginning and ending of a seam should be secured through approximately 3 back-stitches. Back-stitching has to be done exactly on the same line.
- To piece on stitches at topstitching is forbidden, as it looks messy. This applies especially for topstitching on collars, cuffs, pockets, front plackets, front shoulder- and back yoke-seams. If stitching is joined it must be in not visible places, exactly on the sewing line with a minimum 5 stitches over the broken seam and without back-stitches!
- Symmetrical seams e.g. styling or shaping seams have to be exactly equal in form, position and image.
- Easing in fabric must be even, symmetric and in the correct position.
- When closing seams in stretch or knitted fabrics, e.g. shoulder seams of Piqué-shirts, a cotton tape should be sewn into the seam to avoid stretching of the seam and to secure and stabilize the seam in form and length.
- If basting thread is used it must be removed and the stitches must not be visible on the finished garment.
- Sewn-out edges of collars, cuffs, lapels etc. must be "rolled" slightly, so that the seam lays underneath and e.g. under collar or inner cuff is not visible at the upper side (no piping edge!).
- Seams, which have to keep the length and dimension, are stabilized through interlining strips or sewn-in tapes.
- Felled seams have to be sewn correctly with the cutting edges of seam allowances folded in completely. There must not be any puckering, especially on the "biased" edge of the sleeve closing seam.
- For piped seams the cutting edges of seam allowances must be enclosed completely and the piping has to be even in width and without distortion.
- Bar-tucking - the length and width of bar-tucks e.g. for pocket openings must be equal and in the correct position. The stitches must not damage or distort the fabric.
- The finishing corners of piping must not drag and should be in the same width as the piping.
- Overlocked seam allowances must be fringeless, the overlock stitches have to be constant in density and length, and the edge must not roll in.
- Darts must be symmetric in length, depth and form. The final point of darts can be secured through back-stitching, decrease of stitch length or finishing sewing with 2 cm chain stitch. Darts are pressed towards centre front or centre back of the garment.

Button and buttonholes

Buttons und buttonholes

Summary

The majority of buttons for a standard man's shirt are four-hole buttons or sometimes (but rarely) two-hole buttons in mother-of-pearl or mother-of-pearl imitation, because of a cheaper price.
The buttons are produced in clear colours e.g. white, ecru (off-white), anthracite (dark-grey) and black; or they can be dyed in any colour required. Buttons are also available in mixed colours e.g. brown- or grey-melange. Shirt buttons can be with bright shiny lustre or mat; they can have engraved logos or laser engraved name of labels.
For shirts inspired by "traditional costumes" fancy buttons are used e.g. real harts-horn and mock-horn buttons, or buttons which are sewn on with an eyelet, showing ornaments, coat-of-arms or texts on the upper side. These buttons can be in metal, horn or other materials.
For high-fashion shirts buttons are very important accessories and must be selected with great care and good taste. The diversity of button articles and designs is immense. Top-fashion buttons are often bigger in diameter and their price is much higher because of material and workmanship.
Fashion and high-class labels use engraved logos, special forms or extra large buttons as recognition symbol for the brand, e.g. Co. "Van Laack, Germany" has a 3-hole mother-of-pearl button or Co. "Signum, Germany" uses extra big buttons on their shirts.
Buttonholes on shirts are simple lingerie buttonholes with bar-tucks at both ends of the buttonhole (not tailored eyelet-buttonholes), - see diagram drawing below.

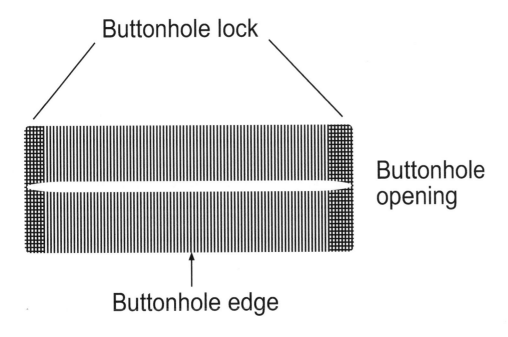

Buttonhole lock

Buttonhole opening

Buttonhole edge

Button sizes

The sizes of buttons are expressed in "lines". This classification comes from the English measurement "inch" = 2.54 cm. 40 lines (symbol is ''') has a button-diameter of 2.54 cm or 25.4 mm = 1 inch. The standard shirt button-size is 18'''. (Please see the chart ending this chapter). In 1981 the German DIN Norm 61576 issued a general metrical table for button-diameters. But this Norm is rarely used and everybody in the shirt business is still using "lines" as measurement for the button-size.

Buttons and buttonholes

For button-down collars and buttoned sleeve-plackets the smallest 14''' buttons are used. Today high-fashion shirts have slightly thicker 16''' buttons for front opening and cuffs.

"Real horn" and "mock-horn" buttons are a little bit bigger with 20''' over 22''' to 24''' diameter; the mostly used sizes are 22''' and 24 line, "fancy buttons" can even be bigger with a diameter of 22''' to 26 lines.

Manufacturing advice for buttonholes and buttons

Buttonholes

The length of the buttonhole depends on the diameter, thickness and surface of the button. As a rule you can calculate the length of buttonhole minus opening = diameter of button + thickness of button + 4 mm, e.g. 18 line button = 11 mm diameter + 2 mm height of button + 4 mm extra = 17 mm or 1.7 cm length of buttonhole.

As buttons can be thicker or thinner, with smooth or rough surface (finish), it is most important to make trial buttonholes in a piece of fabric from production to test that the buttonhole size is perfect (not too small and not too big), before starting bulk production.

To make buttonholes it needs at least two layers of fabric (e.g. Real and Italian placket); "French plackets" have 3 layers of material. If necessary a light-weight band of interlining should be fused on the left front part to strengthen front placket and buttonholes (width of interlining 1 mm less than the width of front placket e.g. front placket = 3.5 cm – width of fusible interlining = 3.4 cm). The length of stitches to sew the buttonhole-opening depends on weaving and material of cloth (fine weave or coarse weave).

Buttonholes are stitched on a 2- thread buttonhole-machine with a knife; the stitching must be close enough that the cutting edge is completely enclosed and no threads are visible. The buttonhole-opening must be cut clean and completely; the knife must not be blunt or damaged (this needs to be checked from time to time).

The bar-tucks at the ends of the buttonhole must not be tight and the buttonhole must lie flat, relaxed and in correct shape.

Buttonholes and buttons must be in the correct position as per instruction or form description and the space between the buttonholes has to be equal (the measurement is from centre of buttonhole to the centre of the next buttonhole). The same applies to the buttons (from centre of button to the centre of the next button). Buttons and buttonholes for front openings have to be in line on the centre front of the shirt and must have the correct distance to the front edge (this depends on width of front placket), e.g. 1.75 cm from the edge for a 3.5 cm wide placket.

Normally buttonholes run vertically exactly on the centre front line of the left front part or front placket. Deviations of this rule can occur through special designs; the factory has to follow strictly form description and sketches.

Some high-class shirt labels want that the last buttonhole nearest to the hem line is cut horizontally. This prevents the front to move up or down; herewith the front placket position is fixed.

The horizontal buttonhole at centre front of collar band starts 2 mm before centre front and runs in the middle of the collar band. The collar-button is sewn on exactly at centre front.

Button and buttonholes

Buttons

Normally, shirt buttons are attached without shank but loose enough to give ease to the buttoned-up front parts. If the buttons are sewn on too tight, it might cause a wavy front placket. This is especially relevant for thicker fabrics like flannels or brushed materials with more volume.
Buttons and accessories e.g. ornaments must be attached securely and be durable for a longer period of time, depending on the kind of garment and the stress of usage; working-shirts are heavier used than an evening-shirt for special occasions.
Buttons should be sewn on with at least 14 stitches, this is dependent on machine and material. The sewing-thread must be tied up inside and not cut off completely, but left with approximately 3 mm length.
In most cases, the colour of sewing-thread is matching to the button colour. The thread colour can also be in a contrast colour e.g. matching to the fabric; this matter has to be laid down exactly in form description or production instructions. **Exception:** Buttons with eyelet are always attached with a sewing-thread in the colour of the fabric.
When sewing on a 2- hole button the stitches should stand in the direction of the cut/opening of the buttonhole.
When using 4- hole buttons in manufacturing it must be clearly laid down if the button is sewn on with straight stitches or cross stitches. The majority of shirt buttons is attached with cross stitch, especially for higher-priced shirts.
Buttons with ornaments, coat-of-arms, logos or letterings should be sewn on that the motive is readable and not up-side-down.
The exact position of button and buttonhole for the collar is crucial. The collar/neckline should form a continuous shape without a step at the front edge. The tie-gap at centre front of collar should be approx. 5 mm or as per instruction. The collar button must sit at the beginning of the buttonhole. The buttonhole has to be so positioned, that front edge and collar form a straight line and the fabric pattern (e.g. stripes or checks) is not distorted.
Normally, there are 7 buttons on the front placket (without collar button). If there are 6 buttons on the front placket of the shirt, the distance between the buttons is larger and the button size should be bigger, dependent on design and length of the garment. The buttons must be in line with the centre front of the shirt and must fit the distance and centre of the appropriate buttonhole.

Button-positions on front placket
The first button is approximately 7.0 – 7.5 cm below collar button or 5.0 to 5.5 cm from collar/neck seam (deviations are possible depending on design or label peculiarity). The distance of further buttons is between 8.0 and 9.0 cm. The gap between the lowest button and finished hemline should be 13.0 to 15.0 cm. For extra long shirts with centre back length of 90 to 95 cm one additional button might be needed.

Buttons on cuffs and sleeve guards

Cuff buttons should be in the middle of height of cuff (dependent on design). There is one cuff button or 2 buttons for "adjustable" cuffs (with a distance of 2.5 cm between the centres of the buttons) – for positions see detail drawings of cuffs. If the sleeve placket/sleeve guard is buttoned, the button position is mostly in the middle of placket opening e.g. a "roof" sleeve-guard is 2.5 cm x 16.0 cm and the placket opening is 13.0 cm, then the button position or the centre of buttonhole is 6.5 cm from cuff attachment seam. The size of buttons for the sleeve placket is 14 line, see detail drawing.

Buttons and buttonholes

Button-down collars

The collar points of button-down collars are fixed onto the front part of the shirt by 14''' buttons. The button position should be reinforced by a small round patch of self-fabric or non-fusible interlining inside the shirt to prevent that the fabric gets torn.
Buttoning of pockets, pocket-flaps, tabs or shoulder-flaps/epaulettes is specially design related and should be shown on precise detail-drawings and in manufacturing instructions.

Manual sewing of ornaments and fancy buttons

If accessories have to be sewn on by hand, the sewing-thread must be only twofold. It is not permitted to use multiple-laid thread. Ornaments or fancy buttons have to be fastened with minimum 5 stitches (twofold). After the sewing process the thread has to be secured inside the garment and the end of sewing thread must be cut cleanly.

Patent or snap fasteners and other accessories

Snap-buttons, rivets, metal rings and other metallic accessories have to be rust-proof and nickel-free (guaranteed by the supplier) to prevent rust-stains or allergies to metallic objects. They must not have sharp edges and they have to be fastened securely and be durable. Size and article of snap fasteners must fit to the material (quality and weight) and the nap-buttons must be fixed with the right machine and at least through two layers of cloth.

Table of button sizes

Diameter in line (''')	Diameter in mm
14	9
16	10
18	11
20	13
22	14
24	15
26	17
28	18
30	19

Button and buttonholes

Spare buttons

Spare buttons should be supplied in case a button is coming off or lost. If there are different button sizes on the shirt, 1 spare button of each size should be provided. Spare buttons can be sewn on outside on the right front placket or inside on the facing of the right front part. They can be attached on the care label, e.g. care label in the left side seam, or the spare buttons can be presented in a small bag as a "special courtesy" to the final buyer of the shirt.

Diagram of possible spare button positions

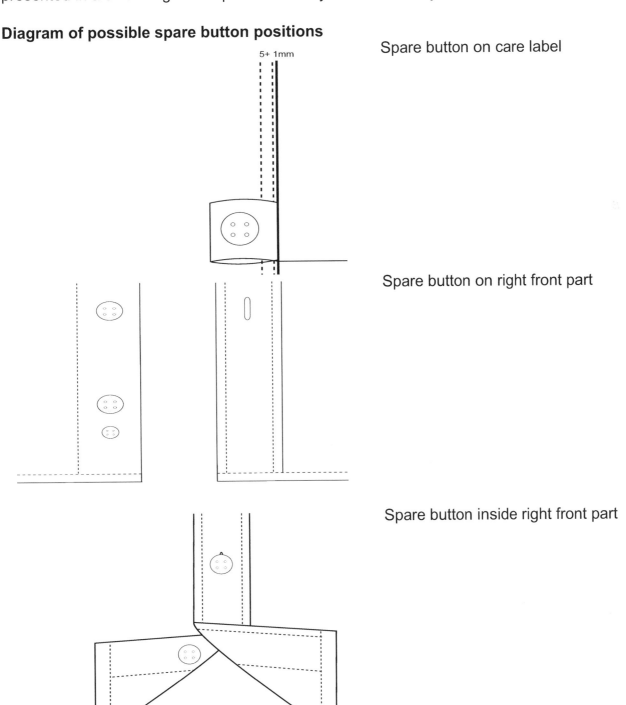

Spare button on care label

Spare button on right front part

Spare button inside right front part

Presentation of men's shirts

Synopsis

„Presentation", stands for the display of a shirt ready for sale. The presentation is a very important point, because the customer in the retail shop pays attention to a product for only 2 seconds (So say the statistic.). In this short time he decides if he is attracted by the shirt, maybe by the colour, fabric or style, and that he is inclined to buy the shirt. If a shirt looks unattractive he will not respond. The presentation is an instrument to "seduce". The 2 main forms of shirt presentation are

- ☞ Folded presentation
- ☞ Hanging presentation

Folded presentation

This is the mostly used form to display men's shirts. As the name says, the shirt is folded on a special cardboard with one or two sheets of tissue paper inside the folded shirt for padding, and other accessories to show the value of the shirt or to give product information, and then the shirt is covered by a poly bag for protection. This kind of presentation is labour intensive and costly. All these accessories are hardly appreciated by the final customer, but taken off and thrown away, when the shirt is unfolded at home. These accessories are expensive, but the shirts look more valuable. The advantage is that the shirts are ready for sale after unpacking from the transport carton. In most cases the price-tag and EAN-code is already on the shirt either on hangtags or stickers. This makes handling and selling in the retail shops much easier.

Hanging presentation

Another way is the presentation on hangers. The ready made shirt is displayed on a clothes-hanger and is packed either on a rail of a hanging transport system or lying flat in a big transport carton. The sleeves are often tucked together at the back with a garment clip e.g. a big plastic clip. Sometimes the shirts are folded in the middle (above waist level); then tissue paper should be inserted to diminish fold lines. This way of transport is called "dead man's folding". Price stickers and EAN-code are also attached, mainly on hangtags fastened with a plastic string through one of the labels (main or size label) or through e.g. the first buttonhole of the front placket. Hanging delivery has advantages and disadvantages. The folding process is not necessary and lots of accessories are not needed, which saves money. Each shirt should be covered by a big single poly bag. During transport on the ship (from Far-Eastern countries it takes up to 5 weeks) the shirts can get creased and perhaps have to be improved on arrival at destination (in Europe labour costs are high). In retail shops the hanging shirts are put on rails, assorted by sizes. Of course some dozen shirts hanging on a rail do not look as valuable as a perfectly folded shirt, maybe presented in a special gift-box.

One big advantage is that the customer has direct access to a hanging shirt and can touch it and feel the fabric. The hanging presentation generates a faster impulse for purchase and is therefore ideal for shops with a big portion of self-service like filial stores or discount markets.

Presentation of men's shirts

While in hanging delivery only one hanger and 1 big poly bag is required, the folded presentation needs a number of accessories.

Presentation of men's shirts

Accessories for presentation

Folding cardboard

Folding sizes of shirts are client specific. Common sizes are 24 x 36 cm or 26 x 34 cm for the finished folded shirt. Depending how stiff or soft the presentation should be, the right cardboard must be selected. The main forms are:

"Full" cardboard for a very stiff presentation, "window" cardboard for a semi-stiff presentation, the "double-T" cardboard for classic shirts (correct but soft display) and the "single-T" cardboard (very soft handle) for casual shirts. The carton weight is around 500 g/m2, the cardboard is usually white in colour and the back is often glossy.

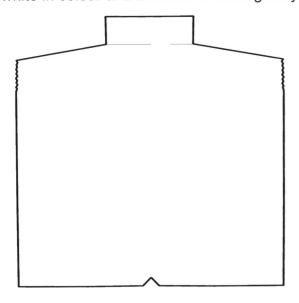

Fulll cardboard

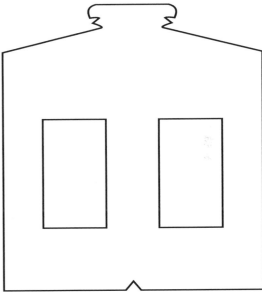

Fulll cardboard with windows

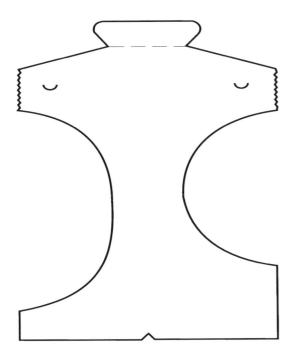

Double asymmetrical T- cardboard

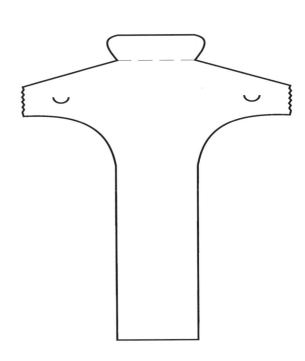

Singe T- cardboard

Presentation of men's shirts

Tissue paper

Between folding cardboard and laid on shirt, tissue paper is inserted. Tissue paper prevents stronger lying pleats and in handling the shirt, there is more volume and the shirt seems slightly padded. There are different qualities of tissue paper e.g. very soft or crackling. For high-class shirts the tissue paper can be printed with the brand name or logo. The paper size is approximately 36 x 50 cm (sometimes 2 sheets are used) or 64 x 50 cm (1 sheet is used and folded one time in the middle).

Pins and garment clips

To fix the folded shirt on the cardboard, small pins or garment clips are used. Nowadays more and more clients do not want the use of pins, as the end-customer could get hurt when unpacking the shirt. Pins can damage fine fabrics. Therefore more often only clips are used to fix the shirt. Garment clips are made in metal or plastic (clear or milky). If metal items are used, they should be rust-proof and nickel-free to avoid rust stains on the fabric during transport or allergy for the customer.

Collar support and collar inlays

The collar is the most important optical element of the folded shirt; therefore it needs special attention in presentation. There is a great variety of objects to support, shape and keep the stand-up collar in perfect form during the long transport to the final customer. Specialized suppliers for garment presentation accessories have big catalogues with all kinds of items, from collar-bones to plastic collar-inlay bands. The following accessories are used to keep a stand-up collar of a folded shirt in shape:

Plastic collar band inlay (collar shaper) with or without anchor;

Plastic collar fly, which is fixed on the collar button;

Paper collar support, a carton strip, which is underneath the collar and not visible;

A special plastic collar band-support under the collar for "Vario" shirts.

These accessories also reinforce the neckline and must be selected according to collar size and diameter of neck hole, and matching to the collar height; e.g. collar band = 3.5 cm at centre back and collar = 4.5 cm at centre back; so the total width of collar at centre back is 8.0 cm. This measurement is divided by 2 = gives a collar height of 4.0 cm.

The variety of accessories is enormous. For example, one specialist supplier for garment accessories offers more than 300 different models of collar shapers and collar supports.

Additionally, there are printed paper collar-inlays with brand names or logos inserted at the back part of the collar band between plastic collar-shaper and shirt. Also printed paper collar "over-riders" are used at the centre back of the collar, indicating the size of the shirt e.g. single size 42, double size 41/42 or L-41/42; and special forms like short fitting, or extra-long and extra-short sleeve and size, and extra-large size. The factory must pay special attention that the correct collar-inlay and over-rider is used corresponding to size, length, sleeve and form.

Presentation of men's shirts

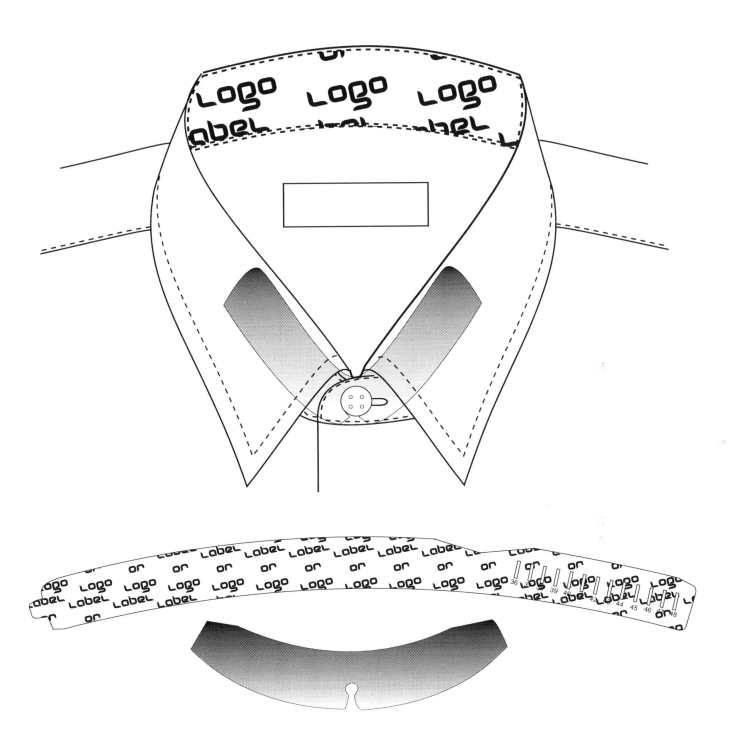

Collar fly and collar band and its position in the collar

Presentation of men's shirts

Poly bag

The poly bag protects the shirt during transport to the final customer. Folded shirts are usually packed in one single poly bag; hanging shirts have one big poly bag per shirt or 1 master-poly bag per lot e.g. 6 shirts are covered under one big poly bag.

Poly bags can be in neutral form (OPP, 30u and printed with the "green dot" and "recycling symbol" at the back side). Or the poly bag is printed with logo, measurement chart and quality related information e.g. "easy care" or "iron-free". The bottom of the single poly bag is usually closed with a self sticky adhesive tape.

 The green dot. This symbol is issued by "Duales System Deutschland" which is in charge of recycling in Germany.

 This symbol is used to indicate that an object is capable of being recycled. One or two characters in the centre show which recyclate has been used.

Additionally in some countries warning notes are requested that "infants or babies should not play with the poly bag to avoid suffocation".

Plastic clothes-hanger

For hanging delivery plastic clothes-hangers are used. The advantage is, handling and display of the shirts is easier in the retail shop.

Additional accessories

Beside the standard presentation accessories like collar inlay or collar fly, many additional items are used. The general instructions and indications of some clients, about how and which accessories have to be used for their shirts are filling pages.

Here are just some examples:

- Measurement chart sticker placed on top of backside in the middle of folding cardboard;
- Tag for extra long-/extra short shirts or sleeves to be fixed at second cuff button or first button of front placket (for half sleeve shirts);
- "Vario collar"-tag to be fixed on the first front placket button (2nd button with collar button);
- "Spare button"-tag to be fixed on the 18'" or 16 line spare button outside of right front part e.g. 7 cm above hemline;
- Info booklet on a black string (length must be 21 cm, that means knotted 8 cm) fixed on the first button of front placket;
- Carton price-tag should be fixed at 2nd buttonhole on backside of shirt with loop plastic string. The length of string is 75 mm and the plastic material is transparent. Price and EAN-code must be visible, showing up-side;
- Product-information card or photo-inlay is placed at back of folded shirt, text or photo must be visible;
- From selling price of 20 EUR on, a soft safety-tag (5x5 cm) should be used to prevent stealing the garment. It is inserted at the back of the folded shirt and placed underneath the button placket inside the shirt. The safety-tag must not stick on the garment and has to be removed before wearing or washing the shirt for the first time.

This list could go on and one has to keep in mind, that every additional item or accessory is pushing up the selling price of the shirt.

Section overview

Part 2: Manufacturing and order handling

Section overview

In this section we will discuss:

- The manufacturing of a man's shirt
- Organizing a production order
- Timing, organization and handling of the shirt production

Grouping of sizes and lots

Grouping of sizes and lots

Synopsis

The grouping of sizes or a lot is the summary of putting several sizes of one article (style) together in one packing unit. The commercial success of a shirt is not only dependent on styling and manufacturing quality, but also upon the right choice of lot.

The rule is that the most popular sizes should have a higher proportion in production e.g. sizes L and XL (middle sizes) are more needed, and less demanded sizes like S or 4XL should be placed in smaller quantity. Commercially unsuccessful sizes should not be placed at all.

The question of the optimal grouping of sizes in one lot depends on different criteria. All these points are interacting with each other.

Which type of shirt? (A high-fashion shirt, a shirt for season sale or NOS-article, never-out-stock);

How/where is the shirt sold? (Chain of retail shops, department stores or mail-order companies);

Which target group of customers? (A younger or older clientele, certain occupational groups e.g. business people etc.).

To give an idea which sizes and what lot should be placed regarding the different target groups of customers, here are 3 examples:

- A high-fashion but lower priced shirt is sold by a chain of retail shops, aiming at younger customers, who want to have top-fashion without paying a fortune. This group is young and probably body conscious, therefore a lot with smaller sizes is appropriate (S-XL); special or bigger sizes are not required or offered in this article.
- A solid flannel shirt is offered by a department store. This model is more suitable for middle aged to older clientele. The customers are likely to be a little bit chubby or have slight figure problems. The lot sizes should be M to 3XL.
- The next style is a classic white business shirt with Kent collar, a NOS-article of a mail order company. Beside in regular sizes M-XXL, this shirt is also offered in S and 3XL + 4XL. Also special sizes with extra short 1/1 sleeves or extra long 1/1 sleeves and extra long body are available in this article.

Grouping of sizes and lots

Some big retail department stores have special ranges for bigger customers. Here the shirt sizes are running from 2XL to 6XL and have a special measurement chart. Styling and proportions have to be adjusted to these big shirts e.g. chest pocket position from centre front of placket and the distance from front shoulder seam to top edge of pocket, the height of back yoke, the position of back side-pleats etc. By placing orders for special sizes one has to keep in mind, that warehouse charges and production costs will go up, as the goods are stored longer, patterns have to be changed and the fabric consumption is much higher. Perhaps one more front button is needed for extra long shirts with centre back length of 90cm to 95cm. These are some of the reasons why high-fashion or lower-priced shirts are not offered in special sizes.

In most cases, the client knows from own experience, market research and previous sales-figures the buying behaviour of his customers and will place orders (sizes and lots) accordingly.

If this information is not available to the reader of this book, the authors give some examples below. These lots are based on a packing unit of 20 shirts per carton.

Sample: high fashion men's shirt

Size	S	M	L	XL	XXL	Total
	37/38	39/40	41/42	43/44	45/46	
Total	2	3	8	6	1	20

Sample: Flannel shirt

Size	M	L	XL	XXL	3XL	Total
	39/40	41/42	43/44	45/46	47/48	
Total	2	6	5	4	3	20

Sample: white Shirt NOS for mail- order
Normal length of sleeve

Size	S	M	L	XL	XXL	XXXL	4XL	5XL	Total
	37/38	39/40	41/42	43/44	45/46	47/48	49/50	51/52	
Total	1	2	6	5	3	2	1	0	20

Extra long length of sleeve and body

Size	S	M	L	XL	XXL	XXXL	4XL	5XL	Total
	37/38	39/40	41/42	43/44	45/46	47/48	49/50	51/52	
Total	1	2	6	4	3	2	1	1	20

Extra short length of long sleeve

Size	S	M	L	XL	XXL	XXXL	4XL	5XL	Total
	37/38	39/40	41/42	43/44	45/46	47/48	49/50	51/52	
Total	1	2	6	4	3	2	1	1	20

Cutting

Cutting

Synopsis

Cutting of bulk production means the cutting of fabric and interlining for manufacturing of shirts according to order, lots and sizes.

At first PP-samples (pre production samples) have to be made and approved by the client. Measurements, workmanship and styling as per design and form description are checked. Washing or lab tests are made to see the fabric reaction, shrinkage of cloth and easy care characteristics.

The rolls of fabric have to be measured and controlled for weaving faults, colour shading or shortage of material. If there are any problems of quality or discrepancy in quantity, the client who placed the order has to be informed immediately by the factory. Also the actual width of usage should be checked, as the self-edge of the fabric can be damaged or distorted and not the entire width of material is usable. This means, there could be higher fabric consumption and the calculation of the shirt (price) is wrong.

Only after approval of PP-samples and the confirmation from the client, bulk cutting can start. The factory must try to keep fabric consumption as low as possible. The pattern pieces are laid out as closely and efficiently as possible, to avoid wastage of material.

A so-called "lay-planning" or "cutting lay-out" is constructed, either manually drawn or plotted-out by a computerized machine e.g. "Lectra-system". Using combinations of 2 or more sizes in "lay-planning", e.g. a small size (M) is combined with a bigger size (XXL), the fabric consumption can be reduced considerably. But this depends on the size-quantity in the lot. Hereafter the number of layers of fabric is pulled on a long cutting table. On the top fabric layer the paper with "cutting lay-out" is fixed, e.g. ironed on and cutting can start.

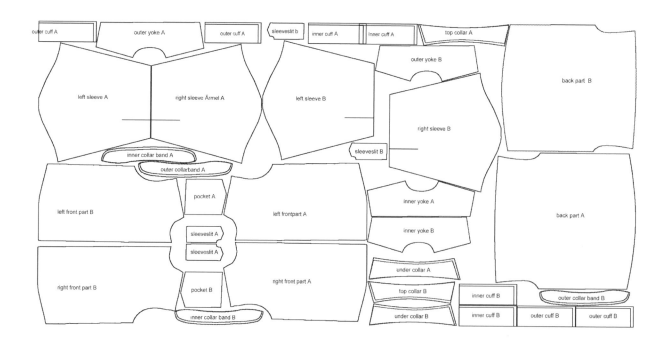

Cutting

Cutting is one of the most important steps of the entire shirt production, and it is, unfortunately, sometimes underestimated. Lots of problems in the sewing-section or some second-quality could be avoided, if the cutting of fabric and especially interlining is more accurate and precise.
CNC controlled cutting automats would be desirable, but in developing countries with cheap labour forces (Bangladesh, India …) bulk cutting is done manually.
When bulk cutting is done manually, it is important that the height of fabric layers is not too high to prevent shifting of material. Patterned fabrics e.g. checks must be cut matching. The front placket should be "blocked-out" (matching of a complete check rapport, when left and right front part is buttoned-up); collar points and cuffs must be cut and worked as a pair; the chest pocket has to be matched to the left front part; the checks on both front shoulders and crown of sleeves should be the same. To avoid distortion and unsymmetrical cuts, checks have to be "spiked" on needles, and if necessary the parts have to be "rough cut" first and "fine or re-cut" afterwards.
To prevent accidents, the cutter should wear a glove of metal chains; very often this rule is neglected because it is uncomfortable and makes working more difficult.

General Instructions

Patterns provided by clients to the factory are not to be changed. The manufacturer must not use original patterns for cutting, but should make copies and markers to use for "lay-planning" and bulk cutting. After using these patterns a few times, they have to be checked for accuracy and, if necessary, renewed.
In principle only perfect and faultless fabrics should be laid and cut. The manufacturer has the obligation to check the fabric on receipt of goods.
All parts of a shirt must come from the same bale of fabric to prevent differences in colour and shading.
The "cutting lay-out" has to take into consideration the actual width of fabric which can be used, as self-edges of material can be damaged.
If the fabric is transparent and stripes or checks are showing through, under- and top-collar, inner- and outer-yoke, inner- and outer-cuff must be cut exactly matching to pattern.

Solid/plain fabrics
In principle fabrics should be cut exactly following the grain-line of warp and weft (woof). To prevent "displacement pucker" on solid-coloured "iron-free" or "easy-care" fabrics, the pattern pieces could be shifted (laid-in) 2° out of grain-line. This option must be clearly mentioned in the production documents.

Patterned fabrics
In striped or checked materials all parts have to be cut exactly following the pattern of fabric; it is not possible to shift parts and running out of pattern; therefore "displacement pucker" might occur.
If the rapport (repeat of pattern e.g. size of checks or stripes) is larger than 4.5 cm, the cutting has to be especially precise, following the fabric pattern. Fabrics must be spiked.
Left and right front part and both sleeves must be cut as a pair. The rapport of fabric must match at centre front, when the shirt is buttoned. The most dominant stripe in colour or texture should be cut at centre front / centre back of body and on the centre-line of the sleeves.
If the fabric has a one-way stripe or check pattern (shadow-pattern), the sleeves have to be turned, so that the stripes and checks are running equal on both sleeves.

Cutting

Prints and Embroideries

Printed or embroidered parts e.g. front plackets, pockets, pocket flaps, inner yokes, collar points etc. have to be "rough-cut" or "blocked-out". The print- or embroidery-position has to be marked precisely in original size (scale 1:1) on the pattern-piece or on a drawing. Later this part is "fine"-cut with a marker.

Prints

Printed logos on casual shirts are fashionable. Traditional woven main labels on the inner yoke of the shirt could be replaced by a "logo-print". The printing position has to be marked on the precise place for a "stencil", as most prints are made by hand-printing with a screen. For printed motives so-called "strike-offs" (trial prints) have to be sent to the client for approval.

Embroidery

The embroidery motive is placed in the exact position on a 1:1 scale drawing. The starting point of embroidery is marked to adjust the embroidery machine. Information about the embroidery should include: (Example)

Design No.:	65400
Picture:	
Name of motive:	"Horse with jockey"
Size of embroidery:	28.4 x 18.7 mm
Starting point of embroidery:	14.1/9.1 mm of motive size (here the needle starts)
Finishing point of embroidery:	14.1/9.1 mm of motive size
Number of colours and needles:	here 1, the motive is stitched tone-in-tone, in one colour matching to fabric colour.
Number of stitches for the motive:	1012 (with 12.7 mm max. length of stitches)
Yarn consumption for embroidery (on top):	3.74 metres
Yarn consumption of under thread:	1.13 metres
Type of embroidery machine:	ZSK

Parts which are embroidered are rough cut, big enough to be stretched into the embroidery frame. The fabric is under laid with interlining and/or embroidery fleece to prevent the cloth to be distorted during the embroidery process. Later the interlining or fleece has to be removed. The final threads of the embroidery stitching-yarn must be cut cleanly and the embroidery should lie relaxed and flat without pucker or tension.

Cutting

Manufacturing advice

Handling of faults

- Cut parts with faults must be sorted out and re-cut. This applies especially for small parts like collar, cuffs, yokes and important optical areas such as front part and placket.
- If quality deviation of fabric or wrong cutting occurs, the client must be informed immediately in written form.

Other hints:

- To assemble shirt parts correctly in manufacturing process, e.g. collar into the neck or sleeves into the armholes, and to fix the correct position for pleats in back part and long sleeves, the pattern should have "notches" and there should be small cuts in the seam-allowances of the fabric parts marking the positions.
- Keep in mind, that fabrics with large pattern rapport have higher consumption of material, if the garment should match perfectly in pattern.
- "Cut on bias"; if parts of the shirt are cut diagonally in stripe or check (cut on bias), the increase in fabric consumption can be considerable. Also manufacturing is much more difficult as diagonal cut materials stretch and there is a higher tendency to puckering.

Review of shirt parts and patterns

Review of shirt parts and patterns

Front parts:

When the front placket of a shirt is buttoned up, the centre front has to match in the complete pattern (rapport) of the fabric. The most dominant stripe of the material, in colour or texture, should be at centre front of left and right front part. Stripes and checks at centre front have to be spiked. The fabric pattern must be the same on left and right shoulder at neck point and armhole.

Back parts:
The most dominant stripe of the fabric should be at the centre of back parts. Stripes and checks at centre back should be spiked.

Collar and collar interlinings:
At collar flaps and collar points of top collar the fabric pattern must run exactly vertical and horizontal. Both collar flaps and collar points give the impression of being mirrored. The stripe/check at centre back of top collar should match to the stripe/check at centre back of collar band. Even if not visible, under collar and outer collar band have to be cut straight in grain-line and must not be distorted.

If collar interlinings are not pre-cut or punched delivered to the factory, the cutting out of bales of interlining has to be extremely precise. The fused collar interlining is the guideline to sew the collar; imperfect cutting can cause unequal collar flaps and collar points and an inaccurate collar edge. (Constructions of collars and collar interlinings are in chapter 4 "Pattern cutting").

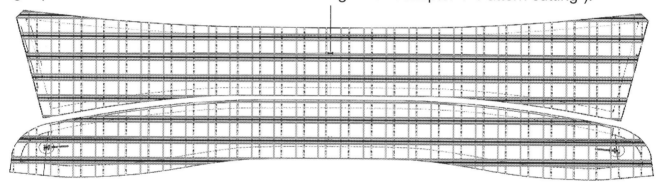

Horizontal cut of collar and collar band

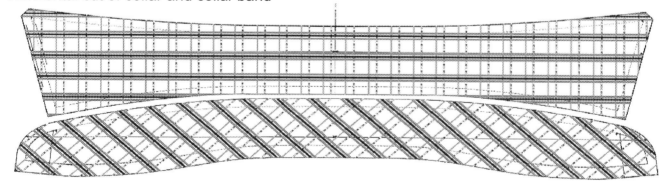

Collar is cut horizontal, inner collar band is cut diagonal (cut on bias)

As fashionable variations, collar band and top collar can be cut on bias. If the top collar is cut diagonal or stripes/checks should run parallel to the front edge of collar flaps, the top collar must be cut with a centre back-seam to match the fabric pattern as a pair at collar points.

Review of shirt parts and patterns

Sleeves:

Sleeves must be cut as a pair and the fabric has to be spiked at centre of sleeve. The most dominant stripe of the fabric, in colour or texture, should be cut at centre line of sleeve.

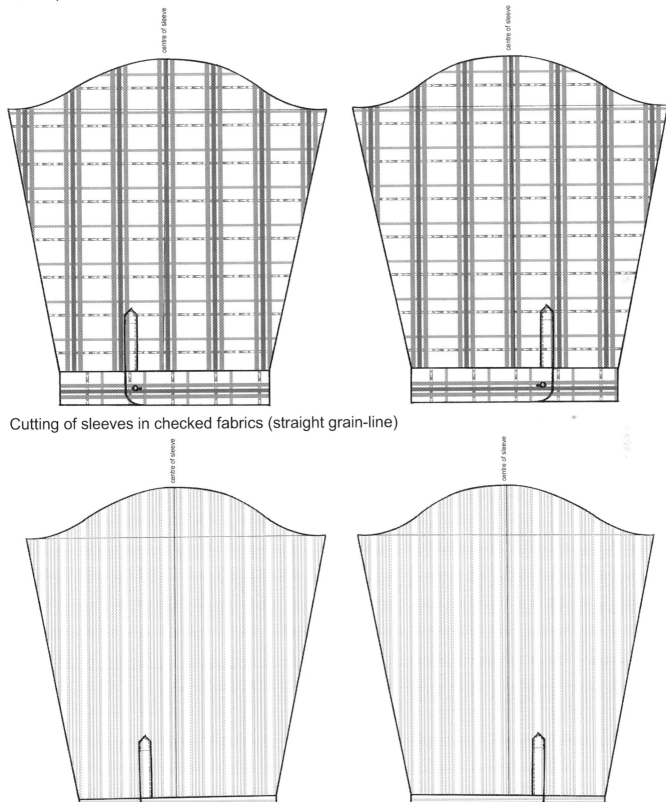

Cutting of sleeves in checked fabrics (straight grain-line)

Cutting of sleeves in striped fabrics (straight grain-line)

Review of shirt parts and patterns

Yokes:

In principle back yokes are cut horizontal to pattern and grain-line of fabric. Outer and inner back yoke seam onto the lower back part must be absolutely straight in the pattern of fabric. Therefore stripes and checks should be spiked when back yokes are cut. At outer back yoke the most dominant stripe/check should be near the yoke seam. The inner yoke has to run straight on grain-line.

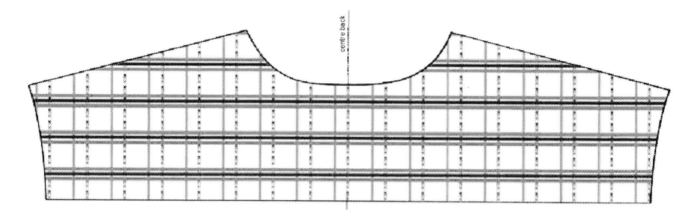

Example of cutting a back yoke in checked fabric

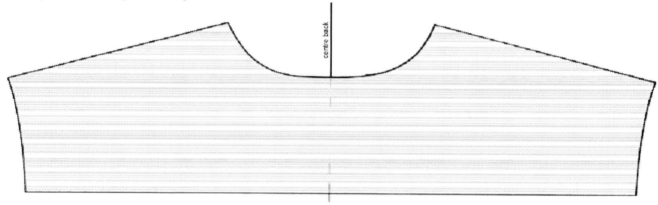

Example of cutting a back yoke in striped fabric

Review of shirt parts and patterns

Cuffs:

Left and right cuff has to be cut and worked as a pair, which means that the fabric pattern at cuff edge and cuff attachment seam onto the sleeve must be identical for left and right cuff. Both outer cuffs must not be separated during manufacturing process. Even if not visible, the inner cuffs also have to be cut straight in grain-line.

Interlining for cuffs:
Outer cuffs are fused with interlining or for textured fabrics like Seersucker fixed with "non-fusible" interlining. Interlinings give a clean and smooth finish to the outer cuff.
The colour of interlining should be adapted to the colour of fabric to avoid colour shading. Fusing recommendations from the interlining supplier should be obeyed, to guarantee that the interlining is fixed properly and will not come loose during wearing and washing the shirt.
Usually the cuff interlining is cut in net/finished shape and dimensions of the cuff. Pre-cut or punched cuff interlinings are preferable, but more expensive. Some top-quality shirts have double-fused cuffs (outer and inner cuff is fused). The price of double-coated interlinings is higher and the manufacturing process much more complicated and expensive (see chapter "double-fused cuffs").

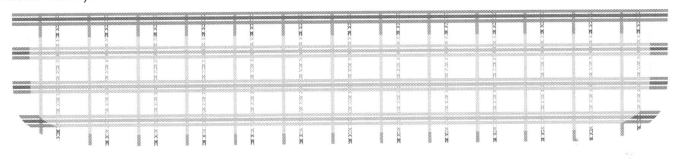

Interlining fixed on the outer cuff before sewing

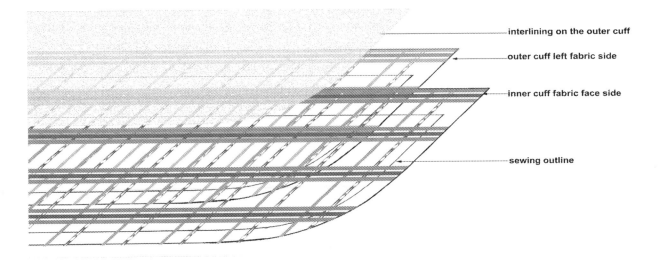

interlining on the outer cuff

outer cuff left fabric side

inner cuff fabric face side

sewing outline

Review of shirt parts and patterns

Pockets and pocket flaps:

If there are no other manufacturing instructions, the chest pocket on left front part (or 2 pockets on both fronts) is cut and sewn matching to the fabric pattern of front part. Special designs can displace the pocket pattern to the front part pattern.

Or the pocket can be cut diagonal (on bias) in stripe or check. If patch pockets are cut diagonally in grain-line, the pocket facing should be re-enforced with a very thin and light weight fusible interlining to prevent stretching and distortion of the pocket opening. In transparent materials a diagonal cut chest pocket might need a lining material, as the pattern (stripe or check) of the front part under the pocket will show through.

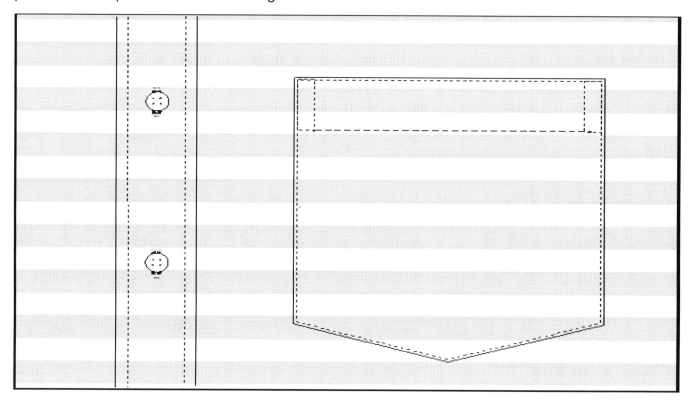

Pocket matches to front part

Review of shirt parts and patterns

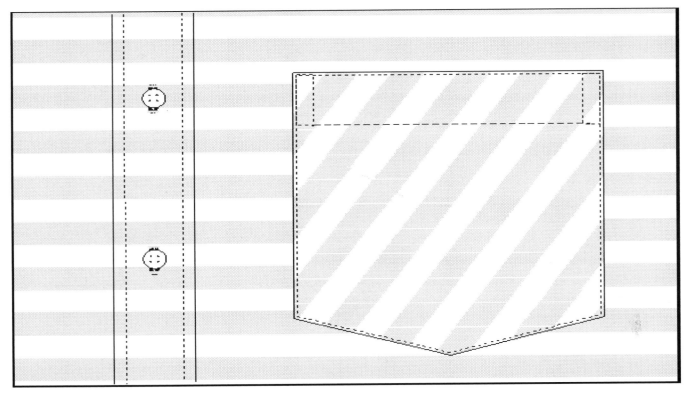

Pocket cut on bias

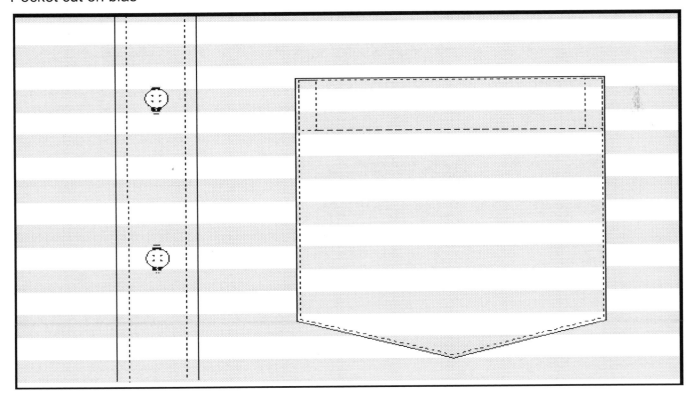

Broadway stripes

Manufacturing of a shirt

Manufacturing of a shirt

Manufacturing preparation

After the cutting lay-out or lay-planning is finished, it is fixed on the top layer of fabric pile and bulk cutting can begin (see chapter "cutting"). Also the interlining parts are cut if they were not delivered in pre-cut form (punched). The fusing of interlining onto the left side of fabric parts follows. The machine park e.g. sewing machines, over lock machines, button and buttonhole automats and others must be cleaned, controlled and set up with yarn and special folder- or sewing-foot. The tension of sewing machine and bobbin must be checked and stitching tests should be made for tension and stitch density. Machine needles and knives in the machines must not be blunt and should be changed if necessary, and so on.

Pre-montage

Before the parts of a shirt can be assembled, detail work on single parts must be done e.g. front placket of front part, pocket, pocket flap, yoke and back part, sleeve plackets, cuffs and collar are sewn, topstitched and ironed. Each single part gets a number on a small sticker for size, same fabric bale and order, that only the correct parts are later assembled to a shirt.

Making of front parts

If a front interlining is required (normally only on the left front part – over wrap of front opening) a ready-cut strip of interlining from a roll, 1 mm narrower than width of placket, is ironed on. It is of the utmost importance to follow stripes or checks of fabric and to keep the interlining in exact position. Then the interlining is fused on the fusing press with the recommended processing data given by the interlining supplier. The front interlining should strengthen front placket and buttonholes, but still keeping it soft and smooth, not bulky and stiff.

Then left and right front placket is turned into an "Italian" or "French" placket and ironed with the help of a carton pattern in width of front placket, sewn and topstitched following design and form description. Most factories have special folding gadgets in different widths of front plackets, e.g. 3.0 or 3.5 cm for a "real placket", on the sewing machine, which sew the placket perfectly and pucker-free with chain-stitch.

After that, left and right front should be ironed and checked for front length, matching of patterns (checks or stripes) and equalized by cutting at hem and neckline.

Then the prepared chest pocket can be sewn onto the left front part.

Manufacturing of a shirt

Making of chest pocket

Usually there is one chest pocket on the left front part. Many variations of pocket shape, pocket facing and topstitching are possible. The position is approximately 21 to 23 cm straight down from neck point of front shoulder seam (depending how far the front shoulder is moved forward, e.g. 4 or 5 cm from HPS and size of shirt) and 6 to 7 cm from centre of front placket. This distance from centre front to pocket position should be graded in groups of sizes, e.g. size S + M = 6.0 cm, size L + XL = 6.5 cm and size XXL + 3XL = 7.0 cm from C.F.

As the pocket must be matched vertically and horizontally to pattern (stripes or checks) of left front part, the following steps are very important and have to be precise. The fabric piece to make the pocket is cut much bigger than the pocket size. The pocket position is marked on the front part with a marker pattern or template and 2 small drill holes are punched 3 – 5 mm (inside) under the final position of the two top corners of pocket. Later the pocket must cover the drill holes completely. This pattern position of pocket on the front part is transferred to the "rough cut" pocket/fabric piece. Then a template / former, in exact size and shape of pocket, are laid onto the left side of the pocket. This template is made from thick carton, or in mass production with one standard pocket form in metal. The seam-allowances of the pocket are ironed around the edge of the pocket former and afterwards cut-by to a maximum width of 1 cm. In round edges the seam-allowance should be trimmed out a little bit more to avoid small pleats and gathering inside, after that the pocket is sewn on.

The pocket facing (straight or pointed, as per design) is ironed down at the top edge/fold line of pocket opening. Then the pocket facing is stitched 1 mm. The prepared pocket is laid onto left front in exact position, covering the marking drill holes and matching stripes or checks of front part. The machinist starts at the top right corner of the pocket, turns front part with pocket and continues sewing 1 mm from pocket edge until she reaches the left top corner. When turning front part and pocket, the fabric must not be distorted; it must lie flat and relaxed.

Manufacturing of a shirt

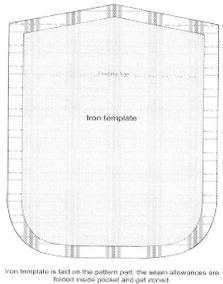

Iron template

Iron template is laid on the pattern part, the seam allowances are folded inside pocket and get ironed.
(View into inner pocket with laid on template.)

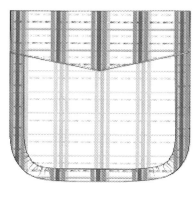

Seam allowances are folded and placket is top stitched 1mm
(View into inner pocket.)

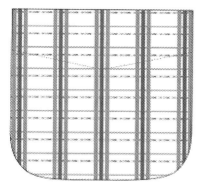

Ready madee pocket, viewe from outside, top stiched 1 mm .

The material of the front part underneath the pocket must not pucker or have fullness. The front edge of pocket has to run parallel in the same distance to centre front. Joining broken sewing / stitching lines is strictly forbidden! The seam-allowances at both top corners of pocket must be turned in and not be visible, after the pocket is sewn on.
The left front with attached pocket is ironed before moving on to the next manufacturing position. If a chest pocket is buttoned, the buttonhole is made in exact position and direction as in form description or detail drawing, before the pocket is sewn on.

Manufacturing of a shirt

Making pocket flaps for a chest pocket

The outer pocket flap is fused with a soft, light weight interlining in finished (net) form of the flap. The interlining is ironed on in exact position and then fused under the fusing press following the processing recommendation of the interlining supplier.

Outer and inner flap is sewn out, just along the edge of interlining, and the seam-allowances are trimmed. At rounded edges the seam-allowance has to be cut out more, to assure a nice curved edge after the pocket flap is turned.

The pocket flap is now turned (face side of fabric is now outside of flap) and ironed. After that the pocket flap is topstitched following design drawing and form description.

If the flap is buttoned onto the chest pocket, the buttonhole must be made now (in correct position and direction).

Now the prepared pocket flap is ready to be sewn onto the front part. The sewing line is 1 cm above the top edge of the pocket (pocket opening). The seam-allowance to attach the flap is maximum 5 mm. The pocket flap is sewn on and both ends are secured with back stitches.

Then the flap is folded down, laying on top of the pocket, and stitched through 6 mm from attaching line. The seam-allowance inside must be completely covered and not visible. The pocket flap should overlap the width of pocket about 2 mm at both sides.

For heavy duty, uniform or denim shirts the ends of stitching can be re-inforced through bar-tucking.

At the end the button is sewn onto the pocket corresponding to the buttonhole in the flap.

Manufacturing of a shirt

Making of back part and yoke

Attaching the woven main label or the making of embroidery with logo at centre back of the inner yoke is one of the first steps in manufacturing a shirt – see the following chapter about "labels and label positions".

Back pleats e.g. 2 side pleats, box pleat or inverted pleat at centre back (see detail sketches) are laid in form following notches and then fixed in position through a short stitching line inside the width of seam-allowance.

Then the back part is sewn between inner and outer yoke. It is important that both yokes are cut straight in grain-line and especially the outer yoke seam must run exactly on stripe or check of the material.

If the yoke seam is topstitched, mostly 1 mm or sometimes with twin-needle double stitching, the outer yoke and the 3 seam-allowances of outer yoke, back part and inner yoke are laid upwards and topstitched. During this operation the inner yoke is laid downwards and not stitched.

Now both shoulder yokes are folded upwards and ironed. Yokes and back pleats must lie flat and no overlapping. If necessary the edges of front shoulder, armhole and neckline have to be cut equal.

Manufacturing of a shirt

Labels and label positions

Main label and size label

The main label, mostly as woven label with brand name or logo, is placed on the correct position with help of a small cardboard template.

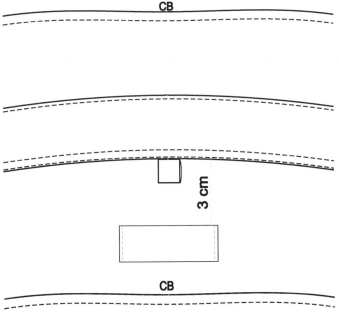

In most cases (drawing no. 1) the main label position is at centre back of inner yoke e.g. 3 cm below neck seam. It must give clear instructions how the label is attached, sewn only on both short sides or attached all around. The folded size label (loop label) is fixed at centre back into neck/collar seam.

Drawing no. 2 shows the main label at centre back but 2.5 cm below neck seam and the size label is attached on the side of main label

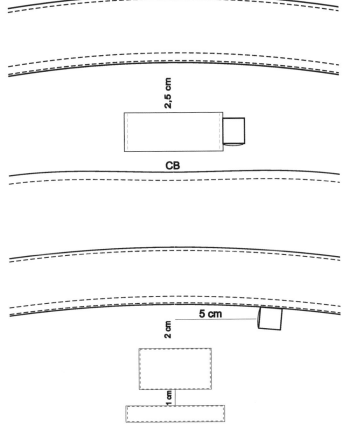

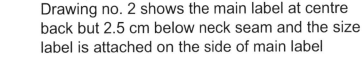

Drawing no. 3 has an additional smaller woven label 1 cm below the bigger main label width special remark e.g. "two ply", "iron-free" or "easy-care". Because of the closer distance of main label to neck seam (here only 2 cm), the size label is moved 5 cm towards the left shoulder. The size label is printed and can carry information like article number and supplier code etc printed on the backside of the loop label.

Sometime, a third label is demanded with information about size, article number or further manufacturer information.

Manufacturing of a shirt

Composition and care label

The label printed with fabric composition, care symbols, washing and ironing instruction can be placed in different positions. Here are just 3 examples:

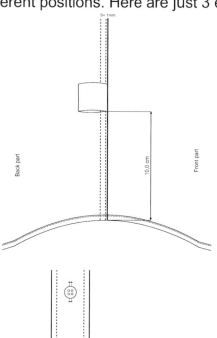

Into left side seam 10 cm above finished hemline.

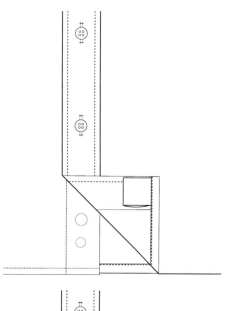

Into the hem of front placket, left front part (over wrap of shirt).

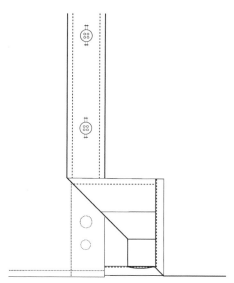

Into the hem of left front part (over wrap of shirt) about 5 cm from front edge

Manufacturing of a shirt

Making of sleeve plackets

Pre-ironing of both sleeve plackets with a template of carton in width of 2.5 cm and length of 16 cm finished, following form description or drawing. The ironed sleeve plackets are laid and handled as a "pair" during the following sewing process.

Sewing of slit under wrap – there are two possibilities:

Either the under wrap is folded in twice times with 3 – 5 mm and sewn on edge from the cuff attachment point to 0 at the upper end of the sleeve slit;

Or the under wrap is sewn out with a piping strip from a folded piece of fabric.

Then the pre-ironed sleeve placket is sewn onto the upper side of the sleeve slit. Most sleeve openings are "roof" plackets (see chapter "sleeve plackets" in part 1).

Now both sleeve plackets are checked regarding total length, equal shape and length of slit opening. After this control both sleeves are ironed. The sleeve plackets must lie flat without pucker in over and under wrap, the end of sleeve slit inside must be clean and all ends of threads cut off.

If the sleeve slit is buttoned, the buttonhole (vertical or horizontal as per design) is made in the middle of sleeve placket and a 14''' button is sewn onto the under wrap.

Manufacturing of a shirt

Making of cuffs

The standard cuff has a fused outer cuff (non-fused for Seersucker and Crinkle fabrics). The interlining is pre-cut (punched) or cut in finished form of cuff (net – without seam-allowance). The interlining is laid onto the left fabric side of outer cuff in precise position, ironed on and then fused under the fusing press, following the processing recommendation of the interlining supplier.

After fusing, the seam-allowance at the top edge of cuff (later attached to the sleeve) is ironed around the edge of interlining and the outer cuff is topstitched from the outside, to hold the fabric allowance inside. Width of topstitching can be 6 mm, 8 mm, but mostly 10 mm and wider (12 – 15 mm). This must be shown on a technical detail drawing of the cuff. The seam-allowance at the top edge must be 5 mm wider than width of topstitching (e.g. topstitching = 10 mm, seam-allowance = 15 mm); minimum 10 mm wide to hold later the inserted sleeve securely.

After that, outer and inner cuff are sewn out, following the edge of interlining and the seam-allowances are trimmed. Then the cuff is turned, so that the face side of fabric is outside, and the cuff is ironed. (The working process is the same as sewing of pocket flap). Then the edge of cuff is topstitched as per design drawing or form description.

Before making the buttonhole and sewing on the cuff button(s), the inside of the cuff must be checked, that there are no loose threads, fibres or dust.

The ready-made cuffs are always handled as a "pair" and must not be separated before being attached to the sleeves later in assemblage (main montage of the shirt).

Manufacturing of a shirt

Making the collar

Preparation of collar

The top collar is fused with interlining; at first lay "basic interlining" on fabric in correct position and fix the interlining lightly with an iron or fusing stick. Then fuse interlining under a fusing press with correct fusing conditions as advised by the supplier of the interlining (temperature, pressure and duration). For "classic Kent-collar", "new, wide spread Kent" and "Shark fin collar" a second reinforcement interlining is required (for placement and dimensions see diagrams). This "collar patch" is also fused as per instructions of the interlining supplier. These three collar types are usually worked with soft "collar bones" or "collar sticks". The inner collar band of a two-piece collar is also fused with interlining. Collar baseline and "collar peak" (also collar nose) are normally cut net i.e. in shape and dimension of the finished collar band. At the top where the collar is attached onto the collar band, the interlining of the band reaches mostly 5 mm into the seam (see diagram of interlining pattern). After the band interlining is placed and fixed on the fabric in correct position, it is fused under the fusing press. For fusing conditions follow again the recommendation of the interlining supplier.

Processing of collar

The top and under collar is sewn out along collar points and collar outer edge; the seam allowances must be cut (reduced), especially at the points of collar, to get equal shape and pattern at the points. Then turn the collar and push the collar points out, but not too hard. After this press the collar by iron, or in industry, with special pressing machines. This operation must be done carefully as the outer edge of the collar has to be perfect and without piping of the under collar (visible).

If collar bones are used, they are now inserted into the collar at an angle of 45° to the collar points. The collar sticks must not be pushed too far into the points, and should be fastened with minimum 3 stitches on each side through topstitching of collar edge. The collar is topstitched as per design or working instructions e.g. 5 mm parallel to the collar outer edge (for design and topstitching details see chapter "Collar"). The side where the collar is joined to the collar band is stitched through with 2 mm. It is most important to check the collar in length, shape and pattern; the collar points must be an exact pair i.e. the collar baseline needs re-cutting if required.

There must not be too much fullness in the under collar and the fabric should not be distorted.

Collar band:

The fabric (seam allowance) at the bottom edge of collar band is turned around the interlining and stitched 5 mm to the fold line. This is the baseline of the inner collar band which is flat stitched to the neck of the shirt. Then the prepared collar is "sandwiched" between inner and outer collar band. The "collar peak" (collar nose) is sewn out with a marker (template) to get the perfect form at left and right front. The width of seam allowance at the base of outer collar band has to be 7 – 8 mm (if necessary re-cut) to match the width of seam in neck hole.

The collar is checked and ironed carefully before it is joined into the neck hole during main assembling process of the shirt.

Manufacturing of a shirt

Assembling process of the shirt (Main montage)

This means sewing the shirt together after preparatory work of single parts e.g. cuffs, collars, pockets etc. during "Pre-montage".

Joining front parts onto back yokes

The back is already attached between inner and outer yoke, with back pleat(s), perhaps loop and topstitching of back yoke seam as per design. The next step is joining the front parts onto the back yoke at front shoulder. If the front shoulder is not intermediate but sewn with safety-stitch (type 504), the seam allowance with over locked edge is visible inside. In this case, if the front shoulder is topstitched, the seam allowance must be laid towards highest point of shoulder and topstitched from the outside as per instruction.

For most shirts the front parts are turned in between inner and outer yoke, and the seam allowances are hidden; this process increases the value and wearing comfort of the shirt. Folding the two yokes and front part in a certain way the machinist needs only one operation for this working process. Then the front shoulder is topstitched through all layers of fabric.

Attaching the collar

After the total shoulder is closed, the shape of neck and armhole must be checked and if required cut by, to get a perfect form without steps. Now the finished collar can be attached to the shirt body.

1st process: The un-fused outer collar band is sewn into the neck hole with 7 mm seam allowance. The front neck curve can be slightly stretched, but there must not be any fullness in the back neck (Easing the fabric in), to prevent puckering under the collar on the back yoke.

2nd process: The inner collar band is flat stitched with 1 mm all around, and then the collar is closed. Slanting and distortion of outer collar band must be avoided and checked after this operation. The machinist must cut all endings of sewing-threads carefully.

It is very important that the sewn-on collar has a clean and continuous baseline without step at centre front, when the collar is buttoned-up. The neck seam should form a right angle (90°) between front edge and collar up to the centre front, and continue into the curve of the front neck. Front edge and collar peak (collar nose) must run in a straight line without recess.

The tie-gap for the tie-knot should be 4 -5 mm at centre front, when the collar button is closed (see illustration in chapter "Collar", 1st paragraph).

Manufacturing of a shirt

Attaching the sleeves

Front parts, shoulder yokes and back part are assembled and the collar is correct sewn into the neck. Now the sleeves can be attached to the shirt body.

Sleeves are attached with "safety stitch" (type 504) and over locked armhole, or they are sewn as "French seam", also called "American seam", and the seam is flat stitched on the body e.g. 10 mm. To operate a "French armhole" the seam allowance at the armhole (body) should be 5 – 6 mm and for the "head of sleeve" (also "crown of sleeve") 18 to maximum 20 mm wide. A special folder foot on the sewing machine turns the seam allowances inside towards each other and the cutting edges of body / armhole and crown of sleeve meet in the middle of the flat stitched "tunnel" (10 mm topstitching). A special rubber-"puller" behind the foot of the sewing machine can improve the quality of this operation. The "French armhole" stitching should be even and clean without puckering and slanting, especially in shoulder area and at the curved lower parts of the armhole.

Closing the side seams

The sleeve closing seam (under arm) continues into the side seam and is sewn as safety seam (type 504) with over locked edge or as felled (lap)-seam. The seam starts at the bottom of the sleeve (wrist, where the cuff is joined) and finishes at the hem on the side of the garment. The seam must be carefully controlled (especially lap-seams) as the shape of the sleeve is tapered and this could cause puckering problems. The side seams of the body are straight in grain line and the danger of distortion is lower. The cross seam under the arm pit must not be displaced.

Attaching the cuffs

The sleeve slits are worked and the sleeves are closed; now the cuffs can be attached to the sleeves. The sleeve is pushed 1 cm into the prepared cuff. The pattern of the sleeve e.g. a check must not be distorted. The outer cuff is sewn onto the sleeve with 1 mm stitching at the top edge of the cuff. The inner cuff should not have too much fullness and the roll at cuff attachment must not exceed 1 – 2 mm. The pleat positions are marked with clips and fixed with a template. The pleats of both sleeves have to be in equal position and distance to the sleeve placket.

Sewing the hem

A straight hem can have wider turnings, e.g. 2 x 1.0 cm folded in and 9 mm stitched from bottom edge. A curved hem (shirt tail) must be narrower, 2 x 0.6 – 0.7 cm folded in and 5 to 6 mm stitching from bottom edge is standard. A special rolling foot for the sewing machine makes this operation easier. Puckering, distortion and tight tension (especially at curves and side seams) must be carefully observed by the machinist.

Manufacturing of a shirt

Making the buttonholes

The horizontal collar buttonhole must run exactly in the middle of the collar band and starts 2 mm before centre front of the collar.

The position (centre) of the 1st front placket buttonhole is 6 – 7 cm below the collar buttonhole or 4.5 to 5.5 cm below the neck seam. It is fixed in form description or manufacturing instructions. Normally all buttonholes are running vertical on the centre front of left front part (middle of front placket). Some brands want the last buttonhole of the front opening in horizontal direction to prevent a distortion when the shirt is buttoned up.

Sewing on the buttons

The buttons are sewn on with "straight stitch" or "cross stitch". It must be clearly stated in the working instructions; also if the buttons are sewn on with the normal stitching thread (colour matching to the fabric) or with a yarn, the yarn colour matching to the button colour. The buttons must not be too tight, but sewn on slightly loose, to avoid a wavy distortion, when the front placket is buttoned up. All buttons must be placed in line and with the same distance.

One spare button of each size and button article should be provided for the final buyer, just in case a button gets lost. The positions where the spare buttons are fixed must be clearly stated in the manufacturing instructions or form description. The spare buttons can be outside (visible) or inside (on facing) of the right front part, e.g. 5 + 7 cm above the finished hem/bottom line of the garment.

Cleaning the shirt

This is an important process before the "finissage" of the shirt. All threads and frays, the beginning and ending of stitching or fibres must be cut and removed. Spots, oil or dirt marks must be cleaned with chemical stain removers or soap. This position should never be underestimated.

Final inspection of the shirt

Now the shirt should look impeccable. Controlling the shirt in final inspection is a very responsible job. The garment must be carefully checked for cutting faults, sewing and manufacturing mistakes, weaving or fabric defects. Any faults discovered in final inspection have to be marked and repaired; or the shirt must be sorted out as second quality.

Final ironing

At first collar and cuffs are ironed. After that side seams, shoulders and back yokes are pressed from the inside of the shirt on an ironing board or ironing table. If the factory is very well equipped, it might have a "Vertomat"; this is an ironing machine (chamber). The shirt is pulled over a "dummy" and buttoned up. This torso is inflatable and 2 arms are extending. Then the dummy slides into the ironing chamber, where the shirt is pressed through steam and heat. It can happen during this process that creases are pressed in, especially on the back and lower armhole area. Then the shirt has to be ironed again on the ironing board. If the factory has no "Vertomat" available, the complete garment must be ironed manually.

Folding, final control, presentation and packing

Now the finished and beautifully ironed shirt can be folded. To avoid creasing, the shirt should be transported hanging (on coat hanger) to the folding table. This special table has a recess for the collar and a metal folding plate. Before folding the shirt, the operator should make a final control, that the garment is clean and perfectly pressed. Folding size e.g. 24 x 36 cm, tissue paper and cardboard (single or double-T, window cardboard etc.) are laid down in form description and manufacturing instructions.

A number of accessories like paper collar support, plastic collar fly, plastic collar inlay, pins, metal or plastic garment clips will keep the shirt in a good presentation form.

Manufacturing of a shirt

The following points have to be observed very carefully:

- The front placket must run straight and without puckering;
- The collar points must be on the same level and in equal distance to the centre front of the garment;
- The right cuff or right short sleeve must be laid forward and fixed in the correct way and position as per instruction or sketch;
- There must not be fullness, puckering or distortion at inner back neck area and inner back yoke;
- There must not be any puckering under the chest pocket.

If necessary the operator has to touch-up the folded shirt with an iron.

Then additional accessories like hangtags, information booklet, photo inlay etc. are attached and the shirt is put into a poly bag, mostly with an adhesive flap at the bottom. Size and quality of the pp-bag are laid down in a trimmings and accessories-list.

During a final inspection the garment is checked for correct labels, presentation form, optical appearance, printing on poly bag e.g. "öko" or recycling symbols, quality reference or measurement chart etc.

Then the shirts are packed in correct assortment (sizes and lot) and quantity into cartons for shipment.

Manufacturing of a shirt

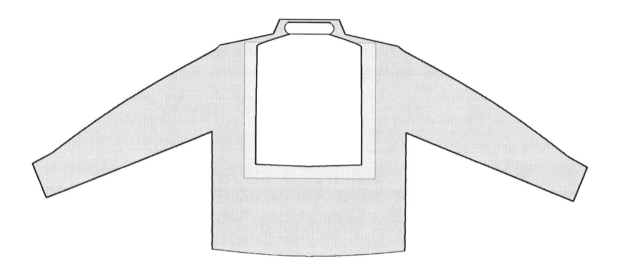

The ready made shirt is laid down to the front side. To avoid pleats a sheet of paper is given over the back. To improve the stability a carton with cut for collar is laid over the paper. The size of the carton will be the size of the ready folded shirt.

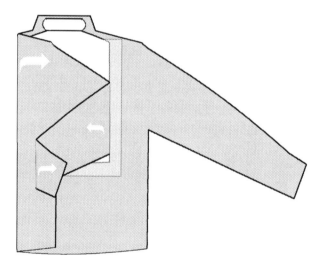

The left sleeve is folded like a „Z" at the edge of carton. Pleats must be absolutely avoided.

Manufacturing of a shirt

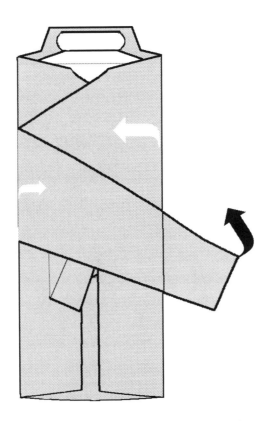

Now the right sleeve is also folded. The point, where left and right sleeve meet is normally fixed with a pin or plastic lip. The right cuff is folded to the front side. There the cuff is fixed inside with a pin or clip. At shoulder the shirt is fixed on the carton with 2 pins or garment clips.

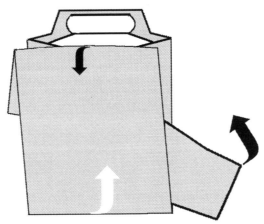

After the sleeves are folded, the rest of the shirt is folded gently inside. Most of the time the lower part of the shirt is tucked in and the top folding edge fixed with pins or clips.

Manufacturing of a shirt

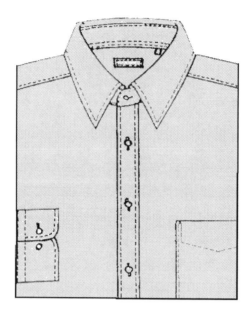

The folded shirt is turned to the front side and the cuff is placed straight on the front part. It is important that the shirt or the pattern runs exactly straight.

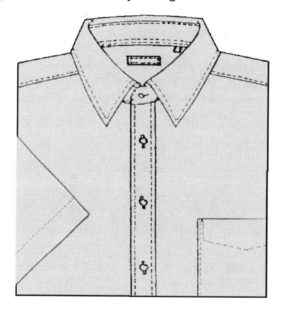

Normally there are no differences between folding long or short sleeve shirts. The main difference is that the half sleeve opening is laid forward as triangle. It is fixed inside the sleeve with a pin onto the right front part of the shirt. The laid forward cuff or short sleeve shows the form of shirt (1/1 arm or half sleeve.)

Stages and order processing production

Stages and order processing in production

Sampling

First of all a prototype sample, mostly in size 41/42 or "L", is produced and thoroughly checked in our own office (agency or buying office). When this sample is satisfactory and without major faults, it can be presented to the final client for approval and confirmation. This pre-production sample (prototype, called PP sample.) is made to control fit and measurements, design details and form, and workmanship. At this stage, most of the time the original fabric and accessories are not yet ready therefore prototype samples are very often made-up in available or similar cloth and substitute accessories.

Mistakes are observed and can be rectified. Also styling modifications can still be made. If there are too many changes a new prototype sample should be requested. Only after perfection of the model-size pattern (here in size 41/42 – L) the grading of all other sizes for this order is done. Then a complete size-set, ideally in the original fabric, is produced. After internal examination the size-set or every second size of the lot can be sent to the final client for approval. Of course only samples without faults are shown to the final client for confirmation.

Parallel washing or lab tests with the original fabric are carried out to test shrinkage and fabric reaction. Care symbols and washing recommendations are supplied by the mill, where this bulk fabric was produced. If the shrinkage data (result of washing test) is too high (up to 2% is permitted) the patterns have to be adjusted before bulk production. This is especially important for enzyme washed casual shirts. Then the "go ahead" for start of production can be given to the factory.

> It is important that all samples are marked as "SAMPLE" before transport, to declare to customs that this is a "garment without commercial value" (Pro-forma invoice). Otherwise customs clearance could create problems and declare the import of the samples liable to duty.

Preparation of production

The more carefully the production is prepared and organized, the fewer problems will occur later in the factory. Trouble during production is avoided and quality secured. Especially when production is placed in cheap labour or developing countries, this point is of immense importance. Working over long distances, communication or language problems, the different levels in education, mentality and attitude of work-force …, make quick intervention and decisions often impossible. Visits to the factories by technicians or quality controllers and staying on location must be planned, organized and used as efficiently as possible, to secure manufacturing and quality of product.

Acceptance of orders/ Checking orders and conditions, confirmation of contract

When an order placed by a client is accepted by the supplier (manufacturer), all points of contract have to be checked and verified for completeness and accuracy (quantity, lot, price, date of delivery, delivery address, packing instructions etc.) Discrepancies must be clarified immediately with the client and after clarification the order is accepted and confirmed in writing. With acceptance of order, a production schedule plan should be submitted by the factory to the client.

Stages and order processing production

Control and supply of production documents

When the final client supplies his own production instructions and documents with his order to us (the agency, buying office), these papers have to be checked carefully for accuracy and completeness. Vagueness, questions and discrepancies must be clarified. If no detailed instructions or production documents were given by the final client, the necessary papers e.g. sketches, form descriptions, manufacturing advice, measurement charts etc have to be provided by the agency.

Material requirement and orders for accessories

The production requirement / accessory list is an important part of production and order documents. It contains all parts necessary to produce and display a shirt. Fabric consumption per shirt, required interlinings, sewing and embroidery threads, labels, buttons, all presentation accessories are listed in article number, quantity per shirt and price per unit with the name of nominated suppliers. Also the total quantity of material and accessories needed for bulk production is calculated. This list provides an exact specification for ordering material, interlinings and accessories, the time of delivery, arrival of accessories and fabric in the factory, and it is the base for price calculation of the garment and planning of production schedule. The so-called "liquid-plan" has to be up-dated constantly and observed. Any changes and new information should be passed on to client, office staff and to the manufacturer.

Supply of all production documentation to the manufacturer

Detailed, clear and precise production documents/instructions are very important when the production is placed in Eastern Europe or Far-east countries. The authors have experienced very often that many problems and difficulties have occurred because the manufacturer has not understood the given instructions and documentation. Or he has misinterpreted the papers. "We are so confused", please explain – is one of the main phrases in the daily e-mail correspondence with Asian suppliers. Just this point could make a trip of the technician or product manager to the production country necessary. The supplier/manufacturer has to confirm the receipt of all order and production documents and that all points are clearly understood.

Bulk production

Systematic controls of factories and production units must be made regularly. A lot of travelling and being abroad is pressed upon technicians and quality controllers. Solution of manufacturing problems or the source of difficulties can sometimes only be found on location.

Delivery / Shipment

The produced shirts are packed and ready for shipment, following production order and delivery instructions. The transport is by truck/lorry (in Europe), ship/vessel (from Far-east) – and if delivery is delayed, the shirts have to be flown by air-freight at the expense of the manufacturer. This important point should be clearly fixed in production order (contract); it can get very expensive

Production documents

Production documents

Synopsis

For improved production planning, better production preparation and smooth handling of manufacturing, the following papers and documents are most important. Once again, the better production is prepared, the fewer problems will arise in sampling and manufacturing.
On principle all documents (drawings, form descriptions, measurement chart etc.) handed out to the factory remain property of the client and should be returned after finishing production, to avoid illegal use. Normally these documents are not given back therefore it is advisable to mark all papers with a copyright sign, especially patterns, technical drawings and important information. Also the remark of prohibition to use the "know-how" and information for other clients should be part of "general terms and buying conditions" under penalty of compensation, if documents are misused.

Plan of production schedule

The following points are fixed in this plan:
Delivery date of fabric, delivery date of accessories and other components for production, date when pre-production samples or photo-samples are needed, period of complete production, date of shipment ex factory and latest arrival date of goods at delivery address.

Guidelines of workmanship

Herein all technical data for production and manufacturing are fixed. The instructions must be as clear as possible without any misunderstanding. These guidelines are **not negotiable**. The points cover among other things:

- Type of seams, seam-allowances, kind of hem and stitching
- Attaching the buttons and button positions
- Topstitching on various parts of the shirt
- Positions of labels

Production documents

Form description

The form description explains the most important elements of the shirt in short form, e.g.

- Type of collar: Kent, New Kent, Button-down, Shark fin, one-piece or two-piece Vario (also "Lido"), wing collar or other forms;
- Form of cuff: Straight, rounded, with broken or cut corners, curved cuff or other shapes;
- Height of cuff and topstitching on cuff;
- Number and size of buttons for cuff, combi-cuff, turn-back cuff;
- Form of sleeve placket: Roof placket, square placket or others – is the placket buttoned? Direction of buttonhole (vertical or horizontal), button size;
- Back yoke: Double yoke, single yoke, "half moon" neck facing, others;
- Back pleat: 2 side pleats (position), box pleat (width), box pleat with loop, inverted pleat at centre back, others;
- Front placket/opening: Real placket, French or Italian placket, or special forms;
- Form of chest pocket: Square, rounded, with broken or cut corners, pointed 5-corner pocket, other forms; size of pocket, cut to match front or diagonal, buttoned etc;
- Type of seam for side and sleeve: Felled/lap seam, safety seam, special topstitching etc;
- Armhole seam: Safety seam, French (also American) seam flat stitched, over locked single stitch seam with 5 mm topstitching etc.
- Shape of hem: Shirt tail (curved) with 2 x 6 mm turning and 5 mm stitching, or straight hem with 2 x 10 mm turning and 9 mm stitching (example);
- Specification of topstitching on: Back yoke and front shoulder seam, front placket (left front) and under wrap (right front), collar and collar band, cuffs, pocket and pocket flap, other topstitching elements e.g. shoulder flaps, styling seams etc. Normally the width of topstitching is indicated in mm, other measurements are usually in cm.

Production documents

Production parts list

This list contains all components needed for manufacturing and production of a shirt, such as fabric article and fabric consumption, sewing threads, interlinings, various buttons, presentation accessories etc. Further useful information are names and addresses of nominated suppliers. Also the total amount of all parts for bulk production of the order and their delivery date ex supplier is needed. Herewith orders can be placed and critical material situations or delivery delays can be monitored and corrected.

Following data should be included in the list of production parts:

- Name and address of client who placed the order
- Order number of client (buying house)
- Date when the order was issued
- Article number and sort of article
- Quantity of article for production
- Delivery of article ex supplier
- Name or number of model/style
- Measurement chart to be used for production
- Necessary pattern (if provided)
- Average fabric consumption and width of cloth
- Composition and construction of fabric

The listing is in the form of a table and can be extended for more details, if necessary.

Measurement chart

Measurement charts are client and customer specific. There are no standard or universal measurement charts for the garment industry. Some brands are cut bigger and more generous, others are smaller cut and slim fitting.
The measurement chart is one of the most important aids for controlling sampling, production output and final inspection. The measurements in the chart refer to the dimensions of the finished, ready-made shirt.
The following example shows a shirt measurement chart set up on pattern related dimensions. The measuring points are expressed with a code. The first letter describes the measuring point in German e.g. V = Vorderteil and the second letter in English F = front part. This measurement chart could be specifically used internationally for English speaking countries producing for the German, Austrian or Swiss markets.

Code	Messbereich/ measuring point	Code	Messbereich/ measuring point
VF	Vorderteil/ Front part	MC	Manschette/ cuff
RB	Rücken/ Back part	PY	Passe/ Yoke
KC	Kragen/ Collar	TP	Tasche/ Pocket
AS	Ärmel/ Sleeve		

Production documents

Sample for a measurement chart; Measurement chart slim fit size

American size symbol		S	M	L	XL	XXL	Tol.
Double sizes		37/38	39/40	41/42	43/44	45/46	
Code	**Measurement**						
AS1	1/1 long sleeve incl. cuff	64.0	64.0	64.0	64.0	64.0	±0.5
AS2	½ half sleeve incl. hemline	28.0	28.0	28.0	29.0	29.5	±0.5
AS3	Elbow width meas. 24-25 from armhole	36.0	37.5	39.0	40.5	42.0	±0.5
AS4	Half sleeve opening	20.0	21.0	22.0	23.0	24.0	±1
AS5	Armhole curved	48.0	50.0	52.0	54.0	56.0	±1
KC1	Collar neckband opening	38.5	40.5	42.5	44.5	46.5	±0.3
KC2	Collar height at centre back (depends on model)	4.5	4.5	4.5	4.5	4.5	±0
KC3	Height of collar band at centre back (depends on model)	3.5	3.5	3.5	3.5	3.5	±0
KC4	Length of collar flap (depends on model)	7.5-8	7.5-8	7.5-8	7.5-8	7.5-8	±0.2
MC1	Length of cuff from edge to edge	26.0	26.0	26.0	27.0	27.0	±0.5
MC2	Width of cuff (depends on model)	7.0	7.0	7.0	7.0	7.0	±0
RB1	Half Chest 2cm below armhole	57.0	60.0	63.0	66.0	69.0	±2
RB2	Half waist 45 cm below HPS	56.0	58.0	61.0	66.0	69.0	±2
RB3	Half bottom/ hem	57.0	60.0	63.0	66.0	69.0	±2
RB4	Width of back at yoke seam	46.0	48.0	50.	52.0	54.0	±1
VF1	Half Chest 2cm below armhole	57.0	60.0	63.0	66.0	69.0	±2
VF2	Width of front	41.0	43.0	45.0	47.0	49.0	±1
VF3	Width of front 18 cm	41.0	43.0	45.0	47.0	49.0	±1
VF4	Half waist 45 cm below HPS	56.0	58.0	61.0	66.0	69.0	±2
VF5	Half bottom/hip	56.0	58.0	61.0	66.0	69.0	±2
VF6	Front shoulder at yoke	16.	16.5	17.0	17.5	18.0	±0.5

Production documents

Measurement Chart normal size

American size symbol		M	L	XL	XXL	3XL	Tol..
Double sizes		39/40	41/42	43/44	45/46	47/48	
Code	Measurement						
AS1	1/1 long sleeve incl. cuff	63.0	63.0	63.0	63.0	64.0	±1
AS2	½ half sleeve length to hemline	27.0	27.0	29.0	29.0	30.0	±0.5
AS4	Half sleeve opening	23.5	24.0	24.5	25.0	25.5	±0.5
AS5	½ Armhole curved	27.5	28.5	29.5	30.5	31.5	±.05
KC1	Collar neckband opening	40.5	42.5	44.5	46.5	48.5	±0.5
KC2	Collar height at centre back (depends on model)	4.5	4.5	4.5	4.5	4.5	±0
KC3	Height of collar band at centre back (depends on model)	3.5	3.5	3.5	3.5	3.5	±0
KC4	Length of collar flap (depends on model)	7.5-8	7.5-8	7.5-8	7.5-8	7.5-8	±0.2
MC1	Length of cuff from edge to edge	25.5	26.5	26.5	27.5	27.5	±0.5
MC2	Width of cuff (depends on model)	7.0	7.0	7.0	7.0	7.0	±0
RB1	Half Chest 2cm below armhole	59.0	64.0	68.0	72.0	77	±2
RB2	Half waist 45 cm below HPS	59.0	64.0	68.0	72.0	77	±2
RB3	Half bottom/ hem	59.0	64.0	68.0	72.0	77	±2
RB4	Width of back at yoke seam	49.5	52.5	54.5	56.5	59.5	±1
VF6	Front shoulder at yoke	18.5	19.5	20.5	21.5	22.5	±0.5
RB6	Length centre back	83.0	83.0	85.0	85.0	90.0	±0.5

Production documents

Measurement chart large for bigger sizes

American size symbol		2XL	3XL	4XL	5XL	6XL	Tol.
Double sizes		45/46	47/48	49/50	51/52	53/54	
Code	Measurement						
AS1	1/1 long sleeve incl. cuff	64.0	64.0	64.0	64.0	64.0	±0.5
AS2	½ half sleeve length to hemline	29.0	29.5	29.5	30.0	30.0	±0.5
AS4	Half sleeve opening	23.5	24.0	24.5	25.0	25.5	±0.5
AS5	½ Armhole curved	31.0	32.0	33.0	34.0	35.0	±.05
KC1	Collar neckband opening	47.0	49.0	51.0	53.0	55.0	±0.5
KC2	Collar height at centre back (depends on model)	4.5	4.5	4.5	4.5	4.5	±0
KC3	Height of collar band at centre back (depends on model)	3.5	3.5	3.5	3.5	3.5	±0
KC4	Length of collar flap (depends on model)	7.5-8	7.5-8	7.5-8	7.5-8	7.5-8	±0.2
MC1	Length of cuff from edge to edge	30.0	30.0	31.0	31.0	32.0	±0.5
MC2	Width of cuff (depends on model)	7.0	7.0	7.0	7.0	7.0	±0
RB1	Half Chest 2cm below armhole	74.0	77.0	80.0	84.0	88.0	±1
RB2	Half waist 45 cm below HPS	74.0	77.0	80.0	84.0	88.0	±1
RB3	Half bottom/ hem	74.0	77.0	80.0	84.0	88.0	±1
RB4	Width of back at yoke seam	58.0	61.0	63.0.	66.0	69.0	±1
VF6	Front shoulder at yoke	21.5	22.0	22.5	23	23.5	±0.5
RB6	Length centre back	85	85	85	87	87	±0.5

Production documents

There are also some differences in pattern parts

Pattern part	Slim fit	Normal fit	Extra large
Height of yoke at CB	5- 7 cm	9-11 cm	13cm
Position of side pleats from armhole	7 cm	9 cm	11cm

Measurements for construction

American size symbol	S	M	L	XL	XXL	Tol.
Double sizes	**37/38**	**39/40**	**41/42**	**43/44**	**45/46**	
Measurement						
Height of front part	24.25	25.0	25.75	26.5	27.25	±0.5
Diameter of neck hole at centre back	7.6	8	8.4	8.8	9.2	±0
Height of back at yoke seam	25.25	26	26.75	27.5	28.25	±0.5
Width of back at chest line	45	47	49	51	53	±1
Diameter armhole	14	15	16	17	18	±0.5
Average height of arm hole	20.5	21.25	22	22.75	23.5	±0.5
Back length to waist	45.25	46	46.75	47.5	48.25	±0.5
Total length at centre back	75	80	80	80	85	±1
Collar opening for size symbol	37/38	39/40	41/42	43/44	45/46	±0

These measurements are normally not part of a Measuremen chart.

Production documents

Sketches and technical detail drawings

A saying is: "A picture says more than thousand words".
With exact drawings and detailed sketches, complicated design and manufacturing processes can be explained easily and without mistakes or misunderstanding. This demands clear and accurate technical drawings. For some parts, like front opening, pocket, cuff, sleeve-placket or collar construction and fusing position for collar interlinings, the technical drawing can be in original size, scale 1:1. Good presentations are especially important, when production is running in foreign countries where language or communication problems, even illiteracy (Bangladesh), can occur.

Patterns and cutting lay-outs

Providing patterns to the manufacturer might be necessary when styles are very complicated or demand new making-up processes, e.g. a new two-piece "Vario"-collar. The client's technician should be in the factory to explain how and in which order the garment is sewn; and he/she should point out, where the critical points in manufacturing are and which mistakes might occur. A small trial production should run, before this new style goes into bulk production.
Here again our advice: All pattern parts should be marked as property of the client.

Prototype sample shirt

It is always helpful, when an actual prototype sample can be provided to the manufacturer together with exact documentation papers, especially if the shirt is complicated in design details.

Shipping instructions

Every client has his own detailed shipping instructions and specifications regarding delivery presentation (form), quantity of lot per box, marking of transport cartons, distribution of shirts after arrival at destination etc. To guarantee a correct and faultless shipment, the supplier (manufacturer) must know all shipping instructions. Complicated carton stickers or printed lists, e.g. packing list etc, should be explained by sending him a filled out sample form of this paper. The people in the factory doing the packing may not be able to read or understand foreign words.

Further advice (important)

Sometimes serious and costly mistakes happen during production, because a wrong measurement chart was used. This happens especially with shirts, which are not regular or standard models or when the final client has different measurement charts e.g. normal, slim or casual fit!
Example: In one order the sleeves should be cut 5 cm shorter (58 cm instead of normal length 63 cm – "extra short"). In the next order the sleeves should be cut 5 cm longer and the body 3 cm longer (68 cm sleeve length and 87 cm instead of 84 cm body length at centre back – "extra long"). **But** the production was cut in normal, regular length! The authors have experienced several such cases, and the financial damage was immense.

- It is strongly recommend to handout separate "Special charts", which are marked largely and clearly: **Attention, recommended Measurement chart - special form for extra long sleeves and body"**

Production documents

Production order

The production order is the placement of contract and the written instruction to the manufacturer to start production. It is also an important document when a LC (letter of credit) is opened. It should contain the following essential points:

- Name (Company) of client, complete address, phone number and E-mail address;
- Name (Company) and complete address of supplier/manufacturer;
- Place and date, where and when the contract was issued; name and signature of the person who wrote and who authorized the order document;
- Order number and reference;
- Information about article, e.g. 1/1 arm men's shirt, quantity of order, price per piece, total volume (sum), currency of payment;
- Material: Fabric composition + construction, width of fabric;
- Short description of article: Sleeve, cuff, front opening, collar, pocket, measurement chart to be used;
- Buttons: Button article, colour, button size(s), total quantity per shirt;
- Yarn: Article e.g. SABA, thickness (Nm 150), colour no: yarn for fabric …yarn for buttons…yarn for embroidery;
- Labels: Main label, size label, care label, extra label;
- Care symbols,
- Additional accessories: Hanger, hangtags, price tag, sticker, info-booklet, cardboard, folding size, poly bag;
- Assortment: Design/colour, article no, colour name, ord. no. final client, sizes, quantity break-down of lot (how many pieces per size), total quantity of lot;
- Packaging: Quantity of packs and distribution;
- Way of presentation: Folded delivery, hanging delivery;
- Samples: When, which and how many samples are needed;
- Delivery: Date of delivery and address of destination;
- Signo: Information on transport carton (see example below);
- Important remark: "Basis of all orders are terms and buying conditions of the client" and "In case of late delivery the goods have to be sent by airfreight on expense of Supplier/ Manufacturer".
- Stamp and signature of authorizing person, signature of office person in charge.

Production documents

Example of carton sticker or stamp

Signo:	STAR
Article no.:	123456
Article term:	Men' shirts
Size:	41/42 L
Colour:	blue
Quantity:	10 pieces
Supplier No.:	4711
Carton No.:	3 - 100
Order No.:	22555/2007

Quality briefing

The quality briefing is an additional safeguard for the client not to receive faulty garments. Also for the manufacturer this briefing gives valuable information how to improve his production quality. All relevant points of faults or imperfection regarding the last production or recent samples are listed, with the advice to avoid these mistakes and to improve the quality. The supplier must confirm the quality briefing in writing. If the mentioned problems occur in the next production, the client has additional evidence to put in a claim.

Special advice

The quality briefing is sent together with the production order to the manufacturer /supplier. Because the client does not want to see the same imperfection again, the following clause should be included:
"In last delivery the following faults were found: (listing). The supplier/manufacturer (name) guarantees, that these mistakes will not occur in the new order, no. "1234".

Another clause is equally important:

☞ "Production order is only valid after signed confirmation of this quality briefing by the supplier/manufacturer". This phrase should be included in the production order. Because the quality briefing is such an important document, the following points should not be missing.

Production documents

Content of quality briefing

- Complete company name and address of client with the appropriate department for quality control in the company
- Date of issue of quality briefing
- Order number and date of production order, and the reference that this quality briefing is part of the production contract

Article data:
- Article number of style/model (from previous production order)
- Term of article and short form description (from previous production order)
- Fabric article, construction, colour
- Reference to measurement chart, which was used for manufacturing

Data concerning supplier:
- Complete company name and address of manufacturer
- Listed supplier number, if available

Data regarding quality:
- Date when the goods were received
- Date of inspection

Listing of quality relevant faults

- Deviation of measurements: All measurements are mentioned which deviate from measurement chart or are out of tolerance. A reprimand should make clear, that all measurements must be kept as per chart or lie in tolerance
- Faults in workmanship: All mistakes which differ or deviate from "manufacturing instructions" or "guidelines of workmanship" are listed in detail. Also here the strong advice, that these faults must not occur in bulk production
- Faults in presentation: If ready made goods show mistakes in presentation or packing, it must be stated, that the final client might refuse receipt of delivery and/or will claim damages, which will be passed on to the manufacturer. Presentation and packing instructions must be obeyed

Further organisational information

- (in clients company) Name of person who is in charge of quality control, telephone number and email address
- Date of issue of the quality briefing
- Signature of quality controller
- Distribution of quality briefing
- Space for signature, stamp and briefing confirmation of supplier/manufacturer

Production documents

Fabric inspection report

Immediately after the arrival of fabrics, the factory should check the material and write a "fabric inspection report". This report is an important paper and should be sent by fax or email to the client within 3 days after the goods were received. Any problems or faults which have direct effect on production are spotted early and measures can be taken accordingly. A quick inspection and detailed report is not only an important protection for the manufacturer, but also a security for the client to claim damages from the fabric supplier!

Faulty materials create a big problem in bulk cutting as parts e.g. with weaving faults or colour shading have to be re-cut manually. As a result of bad fabric quality another critical situation occurs, when the order quantity cannot be produced (short delivery of shirts).

Content

This fabric inspection report should include the following points:
- Name and address of manufacturer
- Name of fabric supplier

Then in form of a list:
- Fabric article number, order number
- Total quantity in meters, according to invoice
- In fact total quantity delivered and measured and the difference quantity (minus/plus) to delivery note and invoice
- Fabric faults: e.g. colour shading in warp or weft, distortion of fabric pattern (stripes or checks) in cm across the material, weaving faults e.g. broken end in weft, thread thickness in warp or weft – slub and knots, foreign fibres in warp or weft (filling), bad selvedge, soiled end or pick, stains etc. Material faults should also be expressed in % of the total fabric quantity.
- It should be mentioned, that the ordered production quantity of shirts cannot be delivered because of fabric shortage or material faults. Fabric cuttings with dominant faults must be sent to the client together with the fabric inspection report as evidence to claim compensation from the fabric supplier.
- Other organisation data: Date of inspection, name, sign and signature of inspector, stamp of the factory.

Section overview

Part 3 Questions of quality

Section overview

Big problems in manufacturing shirts in Eastern Europe or Far-East occur through faulty fabrics, bad workmanship and careless handling/presentation. These problems are guarantees for complaints, claims and return of merchandise.
In this chapter the most frequent quality faults are described. Additionally we offer some solutions how quality problems can be reduced right from the start.

Quality standard and quality management systems

Quality standard and quality management systems

Definition "Quality"

Quality is the existence of all guaranteed characteristics in a product or service.
The exact definition is: "The totality of characteristic of an entity that bears on its ability to satisfy stated and implied needs." (Definition as per EN-ISO 9000 1/1984) If there is a mistake in one or more components of the product, it means a fault in quality.

General view of quality sensitive areas in processing the order

Especially during processing an order, many mistakes can occur and they can run through unspotted to the finished product. These faults will create a lot of trouble, costs and effort at the end. The majority of mistakes happen because of negligence and human error. When problems occur, one should not search for or blame "The guilty person", because many mistakes develop in "team work". Most of the following points could be solved in a constructive, educational and calm discussion. The listed examples are by far not complete, because the variety of mistakes, which can occur, is immense.

Mistakes on client's side
Very often there are inaccurate or vague instructions from the client how to manufacture the shirt (e.g. form and dimensions of collar, front opening/placket, shape and dimensions of cuff, cutting, measurement chart, assortment, presentation, packing and delivery instructions etc.) If the client does not know exactly what he wants, it is impossible for the manufacturer to meet the request of the client. Careful market research is necessary to avoid wrong decisions in planning the collection and placement of production.

Unrealistic production schedule and delivery date
The classic, traditional "Two-season per year" cycle (Spring/Summer and Autumn/Winter Collection) belongs to the past. Vertical retail-chains have changed the system; The season is continuous. Some companies present 4 to 12 collections per year "on point of sale". Also the product "Shirt" is afflicted by this fast rhythm.
But one has to keep in mind, that a shirt production with weaving and finishing of fabric, sampling, bulk manufacturing, presentation and shipping of goods can take up to 3 months or longer. For shipments from Far-East to Europe or USA and customs clearance approximately 35 days must be calculated. To cut delivery time short, the production orders could be placed in Eastern Europe or Turkey, but it is a matter of price. Costs of manufacturing are much higher in Eastern Europe or Turkey, and only high-quality shirts can be produced here; the lower end of the garment market must be manufactured in Far-East. The same applies to fabrics; many shirt fabrics are made in China or Vietnam and the shirts are also manufactured in Far-East.

Delayed and inaccurate control of PP-samples and late response with quality report:
Delays in controlling pre-production samples and taking a long time to send the quality report to the factory, with the necessary advice to correct the mistakes and to improve the quality standard, causes delay in production. As we mentioned in the preceding paragraph, the production schedule is always very tight; therefore delayed sample inspection in the client's quality department and late response aggravates the situation immensely! This might be a bigger problem, if the responsible technician is not in the office, but in a factory abroad and only clerks with little technical knowledge are available to check the samples. Internal training and education of staff is strongly recommended.

Quality standard and quality management systems

Mistakes on producer's side

Incomplete, incorrect or wrong production documents
The most frequent faults occur during production because of incomplete documentation (sketches or instructions are missing), information is out of date (amendments were not passed on to the factory floor), wrong measurement charts were used etc.
These problems cost time and money, and they damage the image of the supplier.
A main reason is, that many administrative people in the office don't have any technical knowledge about manufacturing and working processes. Skilled technicians are essential, also for smaller companies; but they only pay off from a certain size of business. Professional freelance or outside consultants and advisers can improve productivity and quality standards. The factory staff should get permanent internal training and information.

Late transmission of documents
Printing out and sending production documents by mail to the manufacturer takes too long and is economically not justifiable. In times of modern communication it should be normal to transmit all documents, including sketches and drawings by Email.

Lack of internal communication
Again and again difficulties occur when the internal communication in a company fails and important information is not passed on to manufacturer, client or the person responsible e.g. quality controller. It creates a bad image, when the Q.C. is not informed about changes in style or production! The main reason for lack of communication is often outright forgetfulness or simply negligence. In our age with high-tech tools of communication like Email, it's easy to distribute information to all people involved, in real time.

Choice of unqualified manufacturer
(See also special chapter). In times when price negotiations are extremely tough and business partners haggle about few cents per dozen shirts, a cheaper manufacturer might stand a better chance to get the order. But keep in mind that the cheapest is perhaps not the right partner and sometimes untruthful statements are made to get the contract. An attentive check or audit of the factory and the manufacturer is absolutely essential.

Late placement of order for fabrics and accessories
Well before or at the very latest when the production order is sent to the supplier/ manufacturer, all orders for material and components for manufacturing have to be placed, to avoid delays in production schedule. (For further information, see paragraph in chapter "faults on client's side".)

Quality standard and quality management systems

Faults on suppliers side

Bad conditions of the ordered production components see chapter „Quality relevant parts in production"

Late shipment of components
Delays are annoying but sometimes they are not avoidable. The reasons might be:

- Shipment problems by the sub providers
- Delays on shipment
- Problems with custom

It is important to confirm the order exactly to prevent delays.

Faults on manufacturers side

Insufficient comprehension of the production documents
Language problems are a big problem resulting from placing orders in the Far-East. Normally English is the most used language, but unfortunately a lot of manufacturers do not have command of this language. There is also a lack of English lessons in some fashion schools, so that a number of newcomers get into a lot of trouble when handling first orders. Additionally in the Far-East there exists a cultural problem of mentality. The authors were often irritated that the people don't care about some production problems. For example: If a hem is not sewn the people notice this and correct it, but nobody takes care about wrongly sewn cuff or collar. It seems that people don't have faith in these details. Also here training and education is most urgent.

Lack of training and motivation of the workers
What is mentioned in the previous paragraph explains the cause of this problem. There are no training schemes and very few colleges in Far-East countries, therefore the concept is: "Learning by doing". Kids are working as "helpers" (cutting threads and checking measurements or sewing); in doing so, they observe the work of a "semi-operator" at the sewing machine. After some time (maybe few months) the helper can show his/her skills and can be up-graded to semi-operator, later to "operator" or after some years to "senior operator", but he must be able to do 4 to 5 different working processes. Work ethics, or how important each working position is, to get a quality product at the end, is not taught. Doing the same operation from morning till evening and day by day is monotonous, boring and deadens people's sensibility. The workers remain "semi-skilled". It would be helpful to implement intensive training and education programmes, to illustrate that the aim of each working process is to achieve high quality and therefore success for the workers themselves and the company. It might also be helpful to change working positions from time to time. People would gain more experience and interest for the job.

Insufficient sample making
Most problems occur when production documents and instructions are vague and misunderstood. The samples are useless; styling is wrong, workmanship is unsatisfactory or presentation is bad. It happens pretty often that prototype samples show up to 20 mistakes and they have to be corrected; new samples must be made and the entire production schedule can be delayed.

Quality standard and quality management systems

Delay in execution of orders and production
Frequent causes for delay in handling orders and production schedule can be: Late delivery of fabrics, accessories and presentation components (e.g. poly bags, folding cardboards, price stickers, hangtags ...), or when parts of the shirt have to be printed or embroidered outside the factory.
Delays may also occur through natural disasters (flooding, earthquake), religious holidays, strikes, political riots or other unforeseen circumstances. Normally most manufacturers strive to fulfill the orders on time.

Faulty manufacturing
The authors are always astonished, how manufacturing mistakes can happen, even when workers were trained and precisely instructed. Negligence, lack of quality awareness and no sense of responsibility are the main reasons for this problem.

Bad working conditions, disrepair of building, old machines and mismanagement
In developing countries many factories are in dilapidated buildings; the working conditions are degrading with bad ventilation, crammed working space and no air-conditioning.
The machinery is sometimes so old, that it should belong to a "technique museum". Also safety standards are very often neglected. Some conditions are unacceptable and environmentally conscious clients should not produce in these factories. Unfortunately there is not enough money to invest in new machinery and to renovate buildings. The balance of strict audit, maintaining quality standard and still keeping the price target is extremely difficult.

Bad organisation and mishandling in production
The authors often noticed needless long manufacturing procedures, flow of production not optimal or garments were not handled with care. An investigation, talks with the responsible persons in the factory, recommendations and solutions to improve efficiency and quality in factory and production are necessary. A written inspection report or drafting of the minutes is necessary to check improvement of the situation during later visits.

Quality standard and quality management systems

Faults on transport side

Delayed delivery of goods

The ready made shirts are transported by truck/lorry from East European countries or by ship/vessel from Far-East. Transportation by truck takes approximately 5 days and shipment by sea up to 35 days, e.g. from Bangladesh to Europe.

Main reasons for delayed delivery are:
- Delays in manufacturing
- Delays in handling the goods (packing) and customs clearance (corruption)
- Incomplete transport documents
- Use of an unreliable carrier (shipping line)
- Political riots, strike
- Bad weather conditions

The best solution is to appoint a reliable and well established shipping line (carrier) to do the shipment. Additionally the forwarder will handle all the necessary export procedures with a lot of experience. Big carriers have regular shipping schedules which guarantee punctual delivery. If delivery of goods is delayed through mistakes on the factory's side, shipment by air freight might be claimed on account of the manufacturer. This option should be part of terms and conditions of the buying contract and should be confirmed in writing by the supplier.

Damages during transport

Not only delays can ruin the business, also damage of the garment suffered during transport. Humidity, sea air, salt water, condensation and temperatures up to 80° C inside the container and the constant rolling of the ship can damage the goods considerably. Very often hanging delivered shirts must be ironed and corrected after arrival in Europe. If any damage is detected when the container is opened on arrival, the defect must be shown and reported immediately to the representative of the forwarder for damage assessment and to claim indemnity from his transport insurance.

Summary of quality sensitive areas in production

Summary of quality sensitive areas in production

Synopsis

Beside the qualification of people working in production, also other components determine the standard of a shirt; they interact one with another. Additionally workmanship and execution of order is crucial for the final quality. The following listing does not claim completeness; the range is too big.

Faults in fabric

Visible faults are mainly: Broken end, weaving faults especially near the selvedge, foreign yarns and fibres, distortion and stains or spots of all kinds. The only solution is checking the material carefully with a light-box to detect mistakes before cutting. Another problem can be shrinkage after washing, fading of colour and faults in finishing of material. Lab and washing tests help to find out any of these defects.

Sewing thread

Problems can occur because of high shrinkage during the washing process. Other problems are caused by stretching the sewing yarn too much, because the machine or bobbin tension is too high. Later when the yarn relaxes back to original length, seam puckering will occur.

Bad quality interlining

When interlining is not fused properly or not fixed according to the recommended specification of the supplier, the intermediate layer can come loose in part of top collar, collar band or outer cuff and the material bubbles. Bad quality interlining can discolour or shrink during washing process and ruin the collar or cuffs.

Buttons

Cheap or low quality buttons can have many defects, e.g. differences in colour or shape, fading of colour during washing, 4-hole buttons have only 3 holes, cracks in material, buttons break easily under sewing- on machine or during washing and spin-dry process.

Spin-dry faults

Wrong accessories are used on the shirt; the position is not correct; the placement of sewing collar bones is inaccurate, e.g. collar sticks must not be pushed hard and too far into the collar, as they could damage the collar point. The position should be in 45° angle to the collar flaps and collar bones should be fastened with at least 3 stitches on both sides through topstitching of collar edge.

Summary of quality sensitive areas in production

Mistakes in manufacturing

Pattern and measurements

Although when it is instructed in manufacturing specifications, that patterns handed over to the factory must not be altered and the finished measurements must follow the measurement chart, it happens often, that pattern are changed unauthorized in the factory and the measurements are not according to the chart.

Example

A shirt is produced in a fabric with a big check rapport. To reduce the consumption of material and still match the pattern of the check, the width of front and back part is changed for bulk cutting. The finished measurement, e.g. chest, waist, hip… of the shirts are smaller than measurement chart and below tolerance. When the preproduction samples were correct, but the patterns for bulk production are manipulated, the manufacturer must be heavily penalized for compensation. Often garments from this production cannot be sold.

Faulty seams

Frequent complaint and return of merchandise is because of bad sewing and faulty seams. Main faults are here:
- wrong stitching and unclean seam allowances
- holes in the seam
- irregular and puckering seams

Seam pucker

Whereas badly sewn seams, holes and irregular stitching are caused by bad workmanship, seam pucker has mostly technical reasons. When seam pucker occurs, measures have to be taken immediately, e.g. checking the tension of sewing machine, machine needle or transport of sewing goods. Many manufacturers have the bad habit of trying to iron seam pucker clean. At first the seams appear smooth, but after first washing, the pucker returns. Therefore washing test should be done even during manufacturing.

Pucker of seams can be divided into 3 groups; each group has different causes:

Tension pucker

The most frequent sort of pucker is caused by too high thread tension or incorrect thread balance if the bobbin thread is wounded tightly. In both cases the yarn is overstretched. After a while or after washing the thread shrinks to its normal length. Another cause might be shrinking of bad quality thread.

Feed pucker

This problem occurs when the under side of the two fabric layers is transported faster than the upper side. Especially fine and smooth materials are affected by this kind of pucker, because the feed dog has no grip. Also "hard pushing" of the fabric by the machinist can release this effect. Another cause can be too fast sewing speed.

Displacement pucker

This pucker happens, when the stitch density is too close or the needle too thick. Very fine materials and fabrics with special finish have the tendency to pucker, because there is displacement of warp or of weft threads by needle penetration and sewing thread. There are several solutions: The choice of a very fine machine needle, reducing of sewing speed, or the use of needles with rounded point (Ball point or needle type SES). A preventive measure for plain/solid colour fabrics is, to cut the material with the patterns laid in a slight angle to the warp direction (approx. 2°).

Summary of quality sensitive areas in production

Mistakes in topstitching

Main faults are here: Unequal length of stitches, wrong width of topstitching, wavy stitching line, bad tension of thread of visible stitching joints.

Mistakes in embroidery

Main faults are here: Too close or too wide stitch density, wrong embroidery position, wrong colours of embroidery yarn, end of yarn not cut properly; pulling of fabric or wavy embroidery because no embroidery fleece or interlining was under laid; the tension of embroidery machine was wrong.

For "iron free" or "easy care" shirts the use of topstitching and embroidery should be kept to a minimum.

Summary of quality sensitive areas in production

Mistakes with labels or tags
Labels are sewn on slanted, in wrong position or are different from instruction.

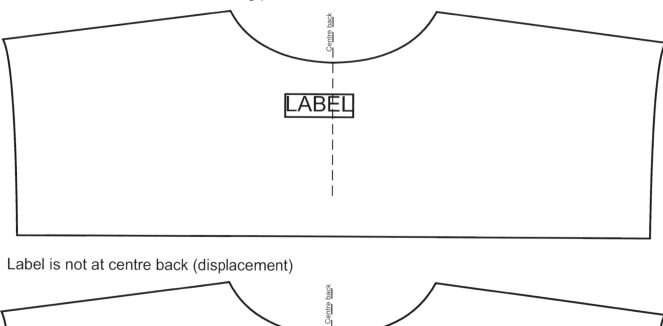

Label is not at centre back (displacement)

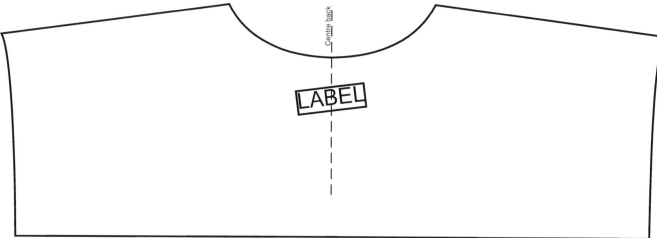

Label is not straight (slanting)

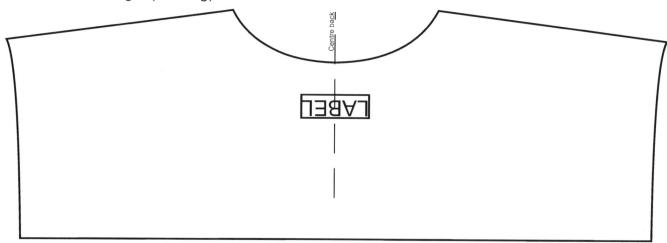

Label is upside-down. This can happen, because people in the factory do not understand what is written on the label or tag.

Summary of quality sensitive areas in production

Mistakes in presentation

Main faults are here: wrong folding size, bad adjusting, front edge not straight; slanting collar, collar point not on the same level and in different distance to centre front (especially noticeable in checked fabric); stains, foreign fibres and loose threads; wrongly placed hangtags and other accessories; use of damaged poly bags.
In the shop, the final customer pays attention for two seconds only, to decide to buy- or just to look. Therefore a faultless and perfect presentation is of utmost importance.

Mistakes during transport

Inadequate packaging
When packing the goods for shipment, sometimes shirts are "chucked" carelessly into the box and the presentation is already damaged before the transport starts. Often the transport cartons are of bad quality, too thin or they are handled roughly during transport. All people involved must be instructed to handle the ready made shirts gently and carefully.

Quality Management System (QM-system)

Quality Management System (QM-system)

Synopsis

As mentioned before, a lot of factors have an influence on the quality of a shirt. Because there are so many criteria, quality management plays a vital role to secure quality.

QM-systems try to detect and solve quality problems during running production. On principle: It is better and more economic to control manufacturing regularly and correct possible trouble spots, than to mend and repair faults at the end of production.

Quality management starts with establishing all quality criteria for the product and style then analysing the smooth handling of orders and specifing the manufacturing process to find out quality sensitive areas.

After that, so-called "procedures" are developed, which should stabilize an equal quality standard, when the working processes are adhered to precisely. QM is not a singular or static program, but must be observed and adapted constantly. Quality and quality management systems are specified in standards DIN ISO EN 9001 to 9004, in theory and practice.

The literature on this subject could fill complete libraries. Also the dissertations, articles and certifications of ISO 9001 – 9004 are nearly endless. Because of the complexity of this topic the book is limited to few examples. On principle:

Quality management is not a matter of working equipment or capital investment, but training and learning process for all people involved in manufacturing the product "Shirt". Everybody must be aware that his/her way of acting and attitude, directly or indirectly, will influence the quality standard!

Quality management in manufacturing

To reach and keep up the wanted quality level is a big problem, especially in the Far-East production. There is no quality awareness in many developing countries and factories proofed and with certificate ISO 9000 are an absolute minority. The authors got the impression, the quality management in some companies existed only on paper.

Important for a successful QM-system are two fundamental convictions:

To be thoroughly convinced, that quality management is important and necessary; it must start at top management level, and run through all administration and production levels, down to the last "unskilled" worker.

An introduced QM is a permanently changing process. The principle of all staff members should be: "What and how is my job at present and how can I improve and do it better?"

Introduction of a QM-system

At first all quality relevant characteristics of a product or service must be clearly and in detail defined and documented.

After that, an investigation about the present situation should follow. It must be examined, to see if the aspired quality standard can be achieved with existing production methods and organization. This examination is documented as a "procedure" and part of a quality management book. Most of the time new, alternative procedures must be developed and tested, until the desired target is achieved. Only then, the optimal procedure is written down for the QM-handbook.

Further steps about composition and organization of a QM-handbook are not explained, because the topic is too complex.

Documentation

Documentation

Synopsis

A complete documentation of all production segments for an order is important to secure quality. It is also part of QM-system following ISO 9003.

Main advantages are:

- The fact, that production procedures are registered in written form, gives client and manufacturer assurance of serious and professional handling.
- The production segments are more transparent.
- Problems are spotted earlier and can be resolved.
- Problems already in process of development can be documented for "evidence". Especially when financial damages occur, collecting of "hard facts" can be crucial for claims.
- Because the complete manufacturing process is monitored, weak points can be improved; this documentation is an immense help in finding solutions for faults.
- It is a critical assessment and guidance where current or further orders may be placed.
- In case of a later claim, the production process can be analysed to find the guilty party.

Disadvantages are:

- Additional workload for persons doing the documentation.
- More bureaucracy.
- It can create a feeling of mistrust on manufacturer's side.
- Considering the pros and cons of the matter, the advantages out-weigh. Using specially provided forms or information technology, the writing and administration work can be reduced to a necessary minimum. The manufacturer must realize that documentation and quality management does not cast doubts upon his competence, on the contrary; it is a very helpful instrument to improve the quality standard in his factory.
- Of utmost importance is that the documentation is complete and all relevant information is available.

Documentation

Execution of documentation

First of all must be established, in which phase of order processing the documentation should begin and who is executing the documentation evidence. It makes sense to start documentation when placing the order; the order contract is already part of it.
Here is an example: Who is responsible for which phase?

Phase of procedure:	Responsible person:
Production preparation	Administrator/ Designer
Sampling	Designer/ Product manager
Production supervision	Technician/ Product manager
Transport/ shipment	Manufacturer/ QC/ Technician

Generally the documentation should be written and accessible to all persons involved, to be able to add further information.

Organisation of documentation

Relevant documents are:

- Order sheet and acceptance (confirmation) of order;
- Complete production/manufacturing documents;
- Complete correspondence;
- Quality reports and test certificates;
- Confirmation of supplier/manufacturer to produce (provide) a product (shirt) according to order and instructions;
- Memos and notes;

A useful document is e.g. a production diary, which contains important information, observations, reports, tests, notes, remarks and correspondence in chronological order, arranged under order numbers. It can be carried on manually in a book (diary) or more efficient as a database, in which all facts can be sorted and programmed. The advantage is information can be handled much easier and quicker.
Other important documents are quality briefing, fabric control report, prototype and production samples.

Standards

Standards

Synopsis

By definition, standards are technical assessments or regulations to standardize material and immaterial objects for the benefit of everybody. Through standardization in production, manufacturing or definition, one anticipates that comparable things or procedures will reach a generally valid, constant and comparable good quality. Standards reflect the up-to-date level of technology. Standardization works like a "guideline with orientation marks" for production and manufacturing. The main target is to make products or services comparable and measurable through definition and unification.

Advantages of standardization

Standardization provides an issue of quality demands for a product or service and gives helpful links for quality management. The certainty of quality for a service/product is established and improved.

Purchasing standardized products is easier and cheaper, as they are comparable.

Acknowledgement of standards provides a legal foundation for disputes between business partners.

Types of standard

Standards can be issued in house (work standard) or specified for a product (industrial standard). Other standards are set up for general subjects.

Many countries have registered own standardization for products; for example: In Germany the register is "Deutsches Normungswerk", which is issued by the German Institute for Standardization DIN (Deutsches Institut für Normung) and accessible to everybody. It is the oldest institute for standardization and works closely with other important institutes all over the world.

International standards are issued for Europe (EN) or worldwide as ISA standard. Most countries give priority to ISA before national standards (in Germany DIN 420), to avoid difficulties in global business e.g. DIN EN and DIN ISA standard.

Use of standards / difference to regulation

Normally all national and international standards are freely accessible. Non-compliance with a standard has no legal effect, except a standard becomes law by legislation; then non-observance would be misdemeanour or crime in serious cases.

In Germany the most important regulation for textile manufacturing is the "Bedarfsgegenständeverordnung" (ordinance on materials and articles) issued on Dec. 23, 1997, in its actual form. Among other things it lays down that the use of dye containing AZO and Chrome VI is strictly forbidden. Another important rule is "Chemikalienverbotsverordnung" (chemical ban regulation) for the use of dangerous chemicals like PCP, Dioxin, Furan, Cadmium, Formaldehyde and others. A true law is the German "Textilkennzeichnungsgesetz" (textile goods identification law for fabrics and fibres). The fabric composition and care of garment must be declared by legal force (care label).

Standards

Other regulations

Beside standards and technical regulations, also import, customs and tax laws must be observed. These are commercial topics which are not discussed in this publication.

Additionally all bigger clients have own delivery, packaging and dispatch conditions which must be obeyed, because they are part of "general terms and conditions". These rules optimise handling and distribution of goods (logistic) for the client according to internal requirements.

For retail shops the principle is:

"The final customer receives the product as it was packed and handled during transport".

Delivery and packing instructions can be pages long, e.g. dimensions of carton, paper quality of carton, quantity of garments per carton, signo, address stickers, maximum weight of carton, and sequence of loading into the truck or container, and a lot more. It is sometimes difficult for the factory and mistakes can occur easily; therefore clear instructions, examples of stickers, marking and placement on the box are most important. Many clients charge claims and penalty fees when packing and delivery mistakes happen.

Grouping of standards

Standards can be classified in groups according to definition:
Basic and general standards;

- Terminology standards – define general terms and technical terminology, e.g. German DIN 60000 handles basic terms and definitions for textiles;
- Product standards – define which demands a product or service has to fulfil to justify the quality criteria;
- Test standards – e.g. DIN EN ISO 105 – A 01 for colour fastness;
- Procedure and technical test standards – these standards specify how tests/examinations should be executed and how the assessment should be done.

The lines between the different groups of standards are fluid. One example: The German DIN 60001 part 1 (definition of textiles made of natural fibres) is a "basic standard", but also a "terminology standard". One should mention that many standards are theoretical and scientific, which makes realization into praticis sometimes difficult. Some tests can only be done in highly specialized laboratories.

Special standard

A special standard is "Öko Tex" standard 100, 101 and 200 of the "International Association for Research and Examination of Textile Ecology". The German partner of this organization is "Hohenstein Institutes", with many international branches. These standards lay down the demands for a textile product to get the certificate: "Textiles Vertrauen – Schadstoffgeprüfte Textilien" nach Öko-Tex Standard 100 = "Confidence in textiles" tested for harmful substances according to Oeko-Tex standard 100". These standards are not part of the German Register of Standards, but they follow the guidelines in definition and testing.

Standards

Relevant standards for the textile and garment industry

The majority of the approx. 200 standards for the textile industry refer to production of fabrics and garments, engineering and textile technology, especially to technical textiles e.g. military textiles used in the production of camouflage fabrics, etc. Few standards specialize in working shirts for miners and fire fighters. There are no special standards for the garment "SHIRT", because patterns and designs cannot be objectively standardized.
Standards are changing constantly therefore just a few most important international standards are listed below:

Relevant Standards for shirt production

ISO number	Issue	Title	Description
8159	1987-04	Textiles; Morphology of fibres and yarns; Vocabulary, Bilingual Edition	Defines the principal terms used to describe the various forms into which textile fibres can be assembled, up to and including cabled yarn. Only contains terms of general application. Terms and/or definitions which are specific to particular fibres (such as hemp, silk, textile glass, metal fibre, carbon fibre, etc.) are excluded
3635	1981-08	Size designation of clothes - part 1: Terms, definitions and body measurement procedure	Is intended as a reference document to be consulted in conjunction with the ISO- Standard for the size designation of clothes applicable to the garment under consideration. Defines body dimensions and describes their measurement.
105-A02	1993- 09	Textiles- Test for colour fastness- part A02: Grey scale for assessing change in colour	Describes the grey scale for determining changes in colour of textiles in colour fastness test and its use. A precise colorimetric specification of the scale is given as a permanent record against which newly prepared working standards and standards that may have changed can be compared. The essential scale (5 steps) consists of pairs of non-glossy grey colour chips (or swatches of grey cloth.). In addition, an augmented scale includes four half-steps and, thus 9 steps.

Standards

105-A03	1993-09	Textiles- Test for colour fastness- part A03: Grey scale for assessing staining	Describes the grey scale for determining changes in colour of textiles in colour fastness test and its use. A precise colorimetric specification of the scale is given as a permanent record against which newly prepared working standards and standards that may have changed can be compared. The essential scale (5 steps) consists of pairs of non-glossy grey colour chips (or swatches of grey cloth.). In addition, an augmented scale includes four half-steps and, thus 9 steps.
105- A01	1995-12	Textiles- Test for colour fastness- part A01: General principles of testing	The document provides general information about the methods for testing colour fastness of textiles for the guidance of users. The uses and the limitation of the methods are pointed out, several terms are defined, an outline of the form of the methods is given and the contents of the clauses constituting the methods are discussed. Procedures common to a number of the methods are discussed briefly.

Standards

105-C06	1997-05	Textiles- Test for colour fastness- part C06: Colour fastness to domestic and commercial laundering	The document specifies a method for determining the resistance of the colour of all kinds and in all forms to domestic or commercial laundering procedures used for normal household articles.
5077	1984-12	Textiles; determination of dimensional change in washing and drying	Applicable to fabrics, garments or other textile articles when subjected to an appropriate combination of specified washing and drying procedures. In the case of textile articles or deformable materials it is necessary to exercise all possible caution in the interpretation of the results.
139	2005-01	Textiles - Standard atmospheres for conditioning and testing	
2859-1	2004-01	Sampling procedures for inspection by attributes- Part1: Sampling schemes indexed by acceptance quality limit (AQL) for lot-by-lot inspection	The document describes a sampling system which gives the supplier the guarantee that lots having a quality level not worse than the AQL reach high probability of acceptance. It is so to be applied to a continuing series of lots. For each sampling plan the corresponding OC- curve is given.
2859-2	1993-04	Sampling procedures for inspection by attributes; sampling plans indexed by limited quality (LQ) for isolated inspection	The document is complementary to ISO 2859 Part1. It describes a sampling system which guarantees consumers protection against a non satisfying quality level of the submitted lots. It is to be applied to isolated lots. For each sampling plan the corresponding OC-curve is given.
2859-3	2006-04	Sampling procedures for inspection by attributes; skip-lot sampling procedures	The standard deals with acceptance sampling for attributes in the case of skip lot in order to minimize inspection efforts.
2859-4	2005-09	Sampling procedures for inspection by attributes; Procedures for assessment of declared quality levels	This standard defines acceptance sampling plans which are ranged by the declared quality level and by the limiting quality ratio.

Standards

9000	2005-12	Quality management systems-Fundamentals and vocabulary	This international standard describes fundamentals of quality management systems, which form the subject of the ISO 9000 family, and defines related terms. The standard is applicable to the following: a) organizations seeking advantage through the implementation of a quality management system; b) organizations seeking confidence from their suppliers that their product requirements will be satisfied; c) user of the product; d) those concerned with a mutual understanding of the terminology used in quality management (e.g. suppliers, customers, regulators.)
9001	2000-12	Quality management systems- Requirements	This standard establishes requirements for quality management systems. Depending on the individual situation the text end of requirements of the draft standard can be tailored in defined limits.
9004	2000-12	Quality management systems-Guidelines for performance improvements	This standard presents guidance for quality management systems. It can be used for all economic sectors when an organization wants to achieve continuous improvement of its processes in order to fulfil the needs of all stakeholders.
15487	1999-12	Textiles: Method for assessing appearance of apparel and other textile end products after domestic washing and drying	The document gives a method for assessing appearance of apparel and other textile end products after washing and drying.

How to find the right manufacturer

How to find the right manufacturer

Synopsis

When placing a production order, a difficult decision is to choose the right manufacturer. There is an immense quantity of manufacturers/suppliers in many production countries, for all quality levels and production capacities. It starts with "production in a garage" with few sewing machines and ends with a top-class fully integrated factory, which can do anything from spinning, weaving, manufacturing the garment up to supplying accessories e.g. labels, hangtags etc.

Criteria of selection

Especially problematic is the situation when orders shall be placed in unknown production countries. The authors experienced that the following points were helpful in selecting a new manufacturer:

- Imposition of client to work with this manufacturer exclusively (no subcontractor is permitted).
- Personal recommendations from other clients, suppliers, agencies or competitors.
- Contacts on trade fairs, seminars or other events.
- Obtaining information and making inquiries at Foreign Banks and Chamber of Commerce.
- Inquiries through an external consultancy.

The following consideration is important to select a potential manufacturer (commercial aspects are not taken into account) so-called "soft skills":
Is this manufacturer (factory) capable (in competence and organization) to manufacture the product I want, in the aspired standard and quality?

Competition in low-price production countries is immense. Manpower and number of manufacturers seem to be unlimited. Many producers promise anything, just to get the order; but many manufacturers overestimate them-selves.
Has this manufacturer produced similar orders and products for a competitor before, and how was the quality? Samples of previous orders are important evidence for assessment.

Personal accessibility
An important but often disregarded point is easy accessibility of the factory in communication and travelling. For example: When a Product Manager or QC travels from Europe to Far-East to visit the factories and check production, high costs are incured for flight, hotel, expenses etc. plus the time factor.

Use of modern communication equipment
Today Email is minimum standard to provide communication between manufacturer and client. Other ways of communication are too slow (letters) or too expensive (telephone, fax). This is of special relevance for productions in Asia. Another advantage of Email is that information can be sent very quickly to all involved persons via a list of all recipients.

How to find the right manufacturer

Responsiveness
A very important point is how quickly a manufacturer/supplier reacts on questions, inquiries, messages or instructions.

How are the production conditions?
As mentioned before, there are factories in every size and standard. Beside technical equipment other points are equally important:
Has the manufacturer a quality management system?
Are environmental issues taken into account in production planning? This point is observed more and more by end customers in Europe.
How is the social situation of the factory workers? Are "starvation wages" paid? Is there child labour in the factory? How is the equipment at place of work?

These points become more and more important, because many non-governmental organisations (NGO) and ecclesial groups are watching the scene and bring bad situations into public awareness, mainly in Europe and North America. A number of companies have expressed their "Corporate Social Responsibility" (CSR) to improve the social situation in developing countries. In the annex there are also some links to this topic.

Will the manufacturer keep the delivery dates?
The rate of delivery and delivery cycle is changing increasingly. Many clients threaten with high penalties for breach of contract if goods are delivered too late, not in the ordered quantity, not in the correct presentation or packing. This applies especially to "timely fix-contracts" or when advertising and sales promotions were launched for the product. The situation will intensify in future. Shipment from Asia takes approximately 30 to 40 days with customs clearance. Strikes or bad weather conditions can prolong the transport. Therefore it might be better to place an order in Eastern Europe for quicker handling and transport by truck which takes just 48 hours. An important aspect in this matter is the willingness of the manufacturer/supplier to send the goods by air freight on his account, in case of delayed delivery.

How production costs should be calculated
Beside sewing charges the costs for pattern construction, perhaps grading, bulk cutting, supplied trimmings or accessories and transport charges must be taken into account for price calculation. For example: "CMT" = Costs of manufacturing, cut, make and trim, or "CIF" = Costs of manufacturing, insurance and freight.
It might be curious to raise the question for costs and calculation at the end of this chapter but one has to analyse all points of this subject to reach an optimal relation between price and service (value for money).
For example: The advantage of low manufacturing costs can be lost through high costs for transport from Far-East or penalty charges when delivery is delayed.

How to find the right manufacturer

Assessment of manufacturer

Assessing a new manufacturer, means to examine that the potential manufacturer /supplier can answer all previous points satisfactory. The building, machinery, facilities, quality of current production, out-put and the atmosphere in the factory are just some aspects of assessment to rate a new manufacturer.

A combination of diverse observations can help:
Personal impression and feeling, behaviour of manufacturer, reactions and inquiries.

The first personal impression and way of acting of the manufacturer

As the saying is "The first impression is decisive". If the factory is in ruins or when the machinery is ready for scrapping a reasonable production is not possible. Honest, straight and sincere behaviour on both sides (client and manufacturer/supplier) is the only sound basis for a successful co-operation and a long time business relationship. If the manufacturer refuses information and inspection of certain production areas, using poor excuses, or when he refuses an audit of his company, you can spare yourself further assessment.

Tour of inspection in the factory

Visiting the factory for examination makes standards evident e.g. cleanliness, condition of building and machinery, conditions of work, working processes and how is the care and handling of the product by the workers?

Self-presentation of the manufacturer (Company Profile)

Most companies attempt to sell themselves with a glossy "Company Profile". It should give information about
Technical equipment (machinery, building, location etc.)
Number of staff
Key figures (legal form of company, turnover, production capacity and quantity)
Reference to current or previous clients in diverse countries

Inquiries

One can get important information from
- Suppliers of fabric and accessories
- Competitors and former clients ("rag-trade" is a big family)
- Credit agencies, debt collecting agencies, the house bank of manufacturer and others

Audit

The term "Audit" comes from quality management and means simplified "Collecting information and assessing systematically with a check list" by audit experts. This check list contains all essential points about production, manufacturing and quality. Because the list is structured systematically and logically, no important item is forgotten and assessment can be done quickly and precisely. It is better when the audit is executed by an outsider who is neutral and objective.

Reference Samples

The manufacturer presents reference samples from other clients in his showroom to prove how good the manufacturing quality in the factory is. Most of the time, these samples are not made in bulk production, but in a special sampling unit.

How to find the right manufacturer

Test Samples

A good way to find out about quality out-put is to get test samples made. When these samples are of poor quality, the bulk production will be even worse! Further co-operation is not recommended.

Trial Production

If the impression of manufacturer and factory is positive, the authors strongly advise to place a trial production to test the factory. The result of a small order of about 200 pieces will prove if the demanded quality standard and co-operation of management can be kept for a bigger bulk production.

Section overview

Part 4 Pattern construction

Section overview

Here, we explain the basic elements of pattern cutting, which measurements are necessary and, step by step, how to draft a shirt pattern from scratch. This example is a comparatively tight fitted "Military/Police"-shirt in size 40.
Also the cutting of sleeves, different collar forms and several ways how to construct back pleats is demonstrated.
However, one should bear in mind that this edition is not a specialized pattern cutting book.

Measurements

Summary

The foundations of garment making are pattern in paper or card board to cut the fabric. Several methods of pattern drafting were developed over many years with the experience of pattern masters and based on arithmetical rules.

Truly, good pattern drafting is an art – a two-dimensional fabric is transformed into a three-dimensional garment; the fit on the body is established and possible technical problems in making-up have to be solved. Changes in fashion, silhouette or even figure deviations must be considered. As a result, this means for the garment manufacturer:

Perfect patterns ensure easy cutting, trouble-free production and a good visual appearance of the garment.

Unfortunately, pattern drafting is not so popular with the students of technical and fashion colleges, because it is not a subject of "free imagination" such as "design" or "fine art", but it's based on knowledge, logic and rules. Nevertheless, it takes a lot of talent, creativeness and a certain touch to translate a design idea or a sketch into perfect proportions, harmonious lines and a comfortable garment. The famous French Fashion Creators are called "Couturier" – masters of cut and silhouette.

More and more today's clothing industry relies on computer aided design-programs (CAD) for design and pattern construction. However, one should keep in mind that the computer is only as good as its operator. He must have the knowledge to execute the work manually if the computer fails, or even to create new forms or programs.

There are several pattern cutting systems worldwide; in Germany and other European countries the method of "Müller & Son", Munich is widely established as standard system for the garment industry. Its special merits are a very good fit and a clear, logical construction method. The following shirt pattern construction is based on this system, mixed with the working experience of the authors.

Construction measurements

Basis of each pattern draft are the construction measurements consisting of "body measurements" plus extra allowances. These measurements influence the silhouette and the fit of the garment.

Body-measurements

These measurements are taken directly on the body. All anatomical distances necessary to make the pattern are measured with a tape measure.

Measurement charts

Since 1970 surveys are carried out, organized by the "German Textile Manufacturing Industry" and "Retail Organisations". Approximately every 10 years 10,000 women, men and children are measured to establish new and up-to-date body-measurement charts. For adults, the participants are between 15 and 65 years of age.

The human body is changing constantly, as the result of life style, food, exercise, sport, health etc; people are getting bigger, taller and older. These changes must be taken into consideration to develop up-to-date size charts for the clothing industry.

The surveys are costly but enable us to establish average standard size charts and also the classification of categories and deviations of figure shapes. A mathematical definition and classification for IT is made possible.

Measurements

Proportion-measurements:

The dimensions of the human body follow certain proportions and rules. Everybody who studies nude or portrait drawing has to learn these rules. When drafting a pattern, attention should be paid to these principles.

The pattern cannot be constructed after the body-measurements. The garment would be like a second skin and one could not move. Therefore, we have to add on extra allowances in certain areas like chest, waist, hip, depth of armhole etc, to make the garment wearable. The degree of additional width or length measurements depends on the fashion-silhouette (how tight or loose should the garment fit the body?) and/or on the type of fabric. Here the experience of the pattern maker is essential.

Finished measurements

These are in fact the measurements of the ready-made garment and they are bigger than the body-measurements. Every garment manufacturer, brand, label… has its own measurement chart. It can vary from very slim fit to extra wide fit. The patterns are drafted after instructions, measurement chart and requirements of the client.

Basic principle

All pattern cutting systems use a grid to draw the construction lines according to the respective pattern drafting method.

We start the construction with drawing a baseline, which form the centre back of the garment and runs from the 5th cervical vertebra to the hem of the finished garment. From this line we develop the pattern to the left, drawing construction lines with length and width measurements after the principle rules of our pattern cutting system. Into this grid we draft the shape of the garment.

Collection size

Most shirt collections are made up in size 41/42 – L (collar/neck size). The constructed pattern is without seam allowances. These have to be added on according to type of seam e.g. safety or lap-seam etc to receive the production pattern for bulk cutting.

Then a proto-type sample should be made up in available fabrics. Measurements as per chart and the workmanship according to form description and manufacturing instructions must be checked. To control the grading from the sample size (L) down to size S and e.g. up to size 4 XL, a complete set of production sizes should be produced. After making the set of proto-type size samples (maybe in available fabrics), pre-production samples in original fabrics and with the original accessories have to be produced, controlled and then sent to the final client for approval, before the bulk production can start.

Example of pattern drafting

Example of pattern drafting

Model: simple man's shirt (uniform style) with 2 chest pockets, buttoned pocket flaps, high back yoke, plain back without back pleats, measurements – size 40 (collar size).

All pattern relevant measurements are in *italic letters*.

Start with the back

On the right side draw a long line = centre back (*CB*) of the shirt, cut on fold and mark the construction starting point "A" = 5th cervical vertebra.

From here measure the following distances:

Height of back yoke (*hby*), here 5.0 cm, a very high back yoke; measurement depends on design (style).

Depth of back (*db*), finished measurement, here 26.0 cm; this establishes the chest line and depth of armhole.

Back length to waist (*blw*), finished measurement, here db + 20.0 cm = 46.0 cm.

Total centre back length (*cbl*), finished measurement, here 80.0 cm.

These distances (points) are squared off to the centre back line (in 90°) resulting in the following construction lines:

Starting point "A" = back shoulder line;

hby = back yoke seam;

db = chest line;

blw = waist line;

cbl = final hem line, length of the finished shirt.

After that, we measure from point "A" along the back shoulder line 1 fifth (1/5th) of the neck circumference (*rsp*), here 40.0 cm : 5 = 8.0 cm; this point is squared-up (90°) and then measure 2.5 cm (fix measurement for all sizes) along the line, and get HPS = highest point of shoulder. Then we draft the preliminary back neckline.

On hby-line we measure the half width of back (*1/2 wb*, here 23.5 cm) and extend the line approximately 0.6 cm to the side for a smoother shape of the back armhole. So we receive the finished length of back yoke (here 48 cm in total). About 12 cm from centre back (around ¼ length of back yoke) we part back yoke and lower back part in taking 1.5 cm out at the back armhole. This is for shaping the back e.g. shoulder-blade.

If the design has a back part with 2 side pleats, the pleats are now constructed at a position of approximately 9 cm from the armhole.

A one-piece back, without a yoke seam, has a relaxed armhole and the 1.5 cm pinch is included in the back armhole circumference.

We measure on the "chest line" (*db*) the half width of back (*1/2 wb*) from c.b. and square up (90°). This line defines the width of the back part and is called "width of back line" (*wbl*). At cross point of back shoulder line/width of back line we measure 2.0 cm down and connect this point with the 2.5 cm raised point at the back neckline. So we receive the preliminary back shoulder and move it (here 2.5 cm) parallel forward; after that we finish the draft of the back neckline from HPS to the final back shoulder and measure from the neck along the final shoulder line the width of front shoulder (*wfs*), here 16.5 cm. The final point is the shoulder point.

Next we measure from width of back line along the chest line the armhole diameter (*ad*), here 15.0 cm; at the end we get the "forward armhole line" (*fal*), squaring this point up (90°).

Example of pattern drafting

Now we half the armhole diameter (2 x 7.5 cm) and square this "side point" down (90°) to receive the preliminary sideline. Around this auxiliary construction line we will draft the final side seam of back and front part.

Further along the chest line we measure from *fal* the half width of chest (*1/2 wch*), here 21.5 cm. The endpoint lays on the centre front line. We square this point off, up and down. This line is centre front and grain line of the shirt. On the centre front line we measure up (from chest line) the height of front (*hf*) = db – 1 cm, here 25 cm and we reach point "B". Point "B" we square off to the right until we cut the forward armhole line (*fal*). From this cross point we measure down 5.5 cm (fix measurement for all sizes) and draw a short 90° auxiliary line.

To draft the front neckline we measure from point "B" to the right Rsp – 1.0 cm = here 7.0 cm, then diagonal Rsp – 0.25 cm = here 7.75 cm and down along centre front line Rsp = here 8.0 cm. With the help of these 3 points we can draw the front neck line as per illustration.

From HPS of front part we measure the width of front shoulder (*wfs*) = here 16.5 cm onto the (5.5 cm down) auxiliary line and draw the preliminary front shoulder. Because we moved the back shoulder 2.5 cm parallel forward, we have to do the same at the front part and draft the final front shoulder line.

Armhole: At first we calculate the "average height of armhole" (*ah*), measuring front shoulder to chest line along *fal* (forward armhole line) and add measurement final back shoulder to chest line, but without the 1.5 cm pinch. Then we divide the total measurement by 2.0 to get the average height of armhole = here 21.0 cm.

Now we construct the armhole. For the back we quarter the *ah* = here 5.25 cm and take this measurement up from chest line along wbl, then we square off and extend this line 0.8 cm to the left into the armhole. This point is the back inset notch to attach the sleeve (*bn*). For the front we quarter ad (armhole diameter) = here 3.75 cm and take this distance up from chest line along *fal*, then we square off and extend this line 1,4 cm to the right into the armhole. This point is the front inset notch to attach the sleeve (*fn*). With the help of these auxiliary construction points it is easy to draft a perfect armhole shape from front shoulder point, over front notch (*fn*) to side point, and further to back notch (*bn*) into back yoke and finally to the back shoulder point.

Next we draft the final side seams of the shirt. From the waistline 0.5 cm up we draw a short auxiliary line and measure 1.5 cm towards centre front and 1.5 cm into the back part, taking out 3.0 cm on the side seam for shaping the garment more fitted to the waist. Approximately 9.5 cm below the waist line the width is reduced by 2.0 cm on top-hip level. From there the side seam runs straight down to the final hemline. If the bottom of the shirt is not straight but curved (shirttail), we measure 4 to 5 cm up on the side seam and draft a rounded hemline as in the illustration, with right angle at the side, centre front and centre back, and a smoothly curved line on the side of the shirt.

Front placket, buttons and buttonholes:

The next step is to construct the front placket and mark the button/buttonhole positions. This shirt has an "Italian placket", 3.5 cm wide, stitched through, with 3.6 cm front facing and 1 cm turning. Parallel to centre front we draw the "over-wrap" of 1.75 cm, then the front facing and 1 cm turning. The first button or the centre of 1st buttonhole is 5.5 cm below the front neck seam. The distance of further buttons is here 9.0 cm; this shirt has 7 buttons/buttonholes for the front opening. Then we mark the position of pockets. A detail drawing in original size (scale 1:1) of pocket and pocket flap with exact dimensions and topstitching is helpful for the production. The pocket flap starts 20.5 cm below front shoulder seam and 5.5 cm from centre front of front placket. The top edge of flap is 2.0 cm above the chest line (see drawing).

Example of pattern drafting

Very important pattern control measures:
To check the finished half chest measurement (½ wb = 23.5 cm + ad = 15.0 cm + ½ wch = 21.5 cm is the half of the finished chest measurement, here 60.0 cm. The total chest for this style in size 40 is 120.0 cm.

Before cutting out the pattern always join together back part + yoke and front shoulder of yoke + front part to control the shape of armhole and neckline; there must be a smooth and harmonious run; also check the finished measurements of width of back, front shoulder and neck circumference following the measurement chart.

To know about sleeve, collar and backs with different back pleat constructions see the following chapters.

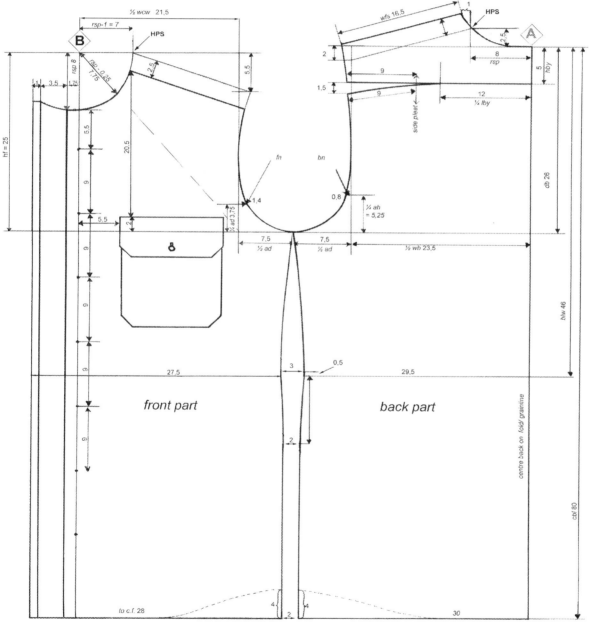

Draft of front and back part pattern

Pattern construction sleeve

Pattern construction sleeve

Summary

To construct the sleeve pattern we need the following measurements:
(Pattern relevant measurements are in italic letters)

Armhole circumference (*ac*): Measure the armhole length of back, yoke and front part, here 50.0 cm;
Half width of sleeve (*1/2 ws*): Calculate ½ ac minus 3.0 – 3.5 cm, here 21.5 cm;
Height of crown (*hc*): Calculate ¼ ac minus 0.5 cm, here 12.0 cm;
Top width of sleeve (biceps) (*tws*): Calculate 2 x ½ ws, here 43.0 cm;
Sleeve length: Total length of sleeve from measurement chart (66.0 cm) minus height of cuff (7.0 cm) = here 59.0 cm;
Length of cuff (*lc*): Take from measurement chart, here cuff length from edge to edge = 27.0 cm;
Height of cuff (*hc*): Take from measurement chart, here 7.0 cm – same measurement for all sizes;
Sleeve placket as design and form description: Here roof placket, 2.5 cm wide 15.0 cm long and slit opening 12.0 cm;
Front and back inset notch: Measure the distance of inset notch to side seam at front and back part of body, here 8.0 cm for the front and 9.4 cm for the back;
Bottom width of sleeve (*bws*): Calculate the length of cuff (27.0 cm) plus pleats (here 1 pleat à 2.5 cm) = 29.5 cm.

The crown or head of a shirt-sleeve is lower than the crown of a blouse, dress or jacket sleeve and it is sewn flat into the armhole, without any ease.

The sleeve construction

We draw a 59.0 cm long middle line = sleeve length minus height of cuff; this line will form the middle of the sleeve and the grain line. Top and bottom of this line is squared off to both sides. The top line is the crown line and we measure from starting point to the left and to the right 21.5 cm (*1/2 ws*). The 2 endpoints are squared down and we measure 12.0 cm (height of crown). Then we connect these two points and get the top width line of the sleeve (*tws = 43.0 cm*).
On the squared off bottom line we measure the half of *bws* to the left and to the right side (2 x 14.75 cm). The right half will be the back of the sleeve; it is divided into equal halves (1/4 of 29.5 cm) and sleeve pleat and the cutting line for the sleeve slit is drafted as in our presentation. The sleeve slit must run parallel to the sleeve grain line.
Two auxiliary straight sidelines are drawn from the endpoints of top width line down to the endpoints of bottom width line. Approximately 24 – 25 cm from the top width line is the position of elbow line and we extend this line 0.5 cm at both sides. Then we draw the under sleeve/side seam with a light curve as in our presentation. To construct the head of sleeve we connect the starting point on the middle line with the two endpoints of top width line. Then these 2 temporary lines are divided into two parts and at these points auxiliary measurements are set up as follows (from the front to the back): 0.4 cm inside, 1.0 cm outside, starting point/top of sleeve. 1.5 cm outside and approximately 0.75 cm outside. These construction points help to draft the crown of sleeve as in our presentation. After that, we mark the positions of front and back inset notch, and the meeting point of front shoulder to the sleeve.

Pattern construction sleeve

To make sure that the head of sleeve has the same measurement as the armhole circumference in shirt body, the constructed crown of sleeve should be measured, compared with the armhole circumference measurement and corrected, if necessary.
Now cuff and sleeve placket are drafted as in design and form description.

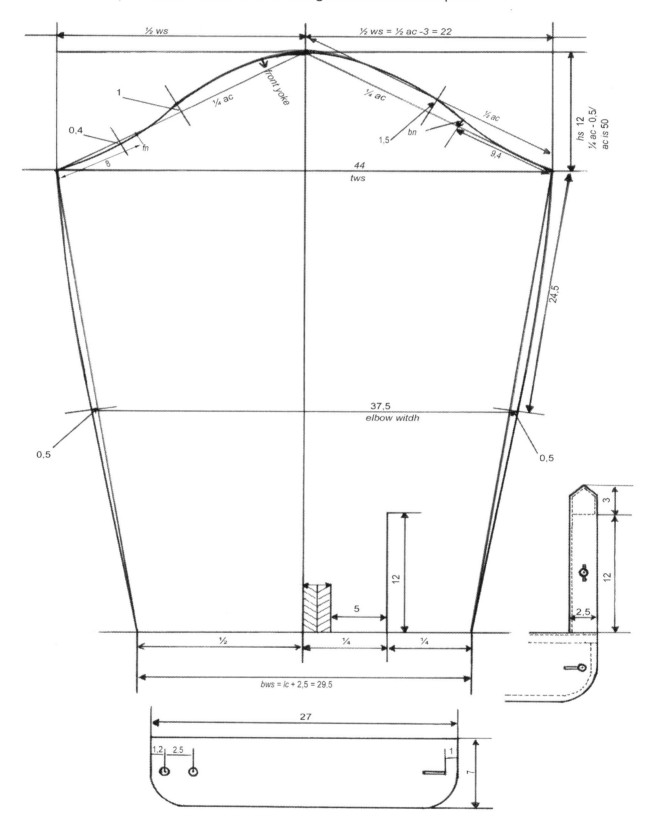

Collar construction

Collar construction

One-piece shirt collar

At starting point **A** we draw a right angle (90°). Around the horizontal line we draft the collar baseline; the vertical side will become the centre back of collar. From A to the right, along the horizontal line we measure the half neck circumference, taken from the body neck measurement – centre front to c.f. (here 20.0 cm). The end point is squared up (90°). Then we half the 20.0 cm distance (10.0 cm) and quarter the front half (2 x 5.0 cm).

From A up along the vertical side we measure 1.5 cm to raise the collar baseline. This amount can be from 1.0 cm to 2.0 cm (the higher this measurement is, the more curved will be collar baseline and collar outer edge). Then we measure the centre back height of collar (cbh), here collar band to break line = 3.2 cm + collar = 4.5 cm, total height 7.7 cm c.b. Collar outer edge, the break line and the collar baseline are squared off in 90° to centre back line. Now we draft the collar base as illustrated, we extend collar wrap, here 1.75 cm over centre front, fitting a front placket of 3.5 cm, and draw the rounded shape of collar peak or collar nose as shown. The front point of collar peak is raised by 0.5 cm and squared of. The centre front line of collar runs parallel to front edge. The buttonhole position is in the middle of collar band and begins 2 mm before centre front. The starting point of collar flap lies 2 mm behind centre front to attain a tie gap of 4 to 5 mm at centre front, when the collar is closed. The collar flap is 7.5 cm long and the collar point is 1.5 cm laid forward. After that we draft the collar outer edge as illustrated.

The collar break line is an imaginary line, which can be indicated through a dotted line. Here the collar interlining is cut out 5 mm for a better roll or break of the collar. Through raising and curved shaping of collar baseline the actual length is approximately 0.5 cm longer, here 20.5 cm from centre back to centre front. Therefore the finished collar length for size 39/40 or M is 40.5 to 41.0 cm.

Neck circumference of body and the final collar length should be measured and adjusted, to make the manufacturing process (attaching the collar into the neckline) easier. Shoulder notches help the operator to attach the collar correctly without distortion of front and back.

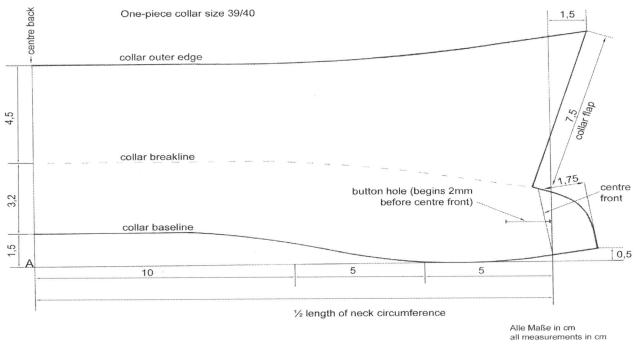

½ length of neck circumference

Alle Maße in cm
all measurements in cm

Collar construction

Two-piece shirt collar

We construct only half of the collar from centre front to centre back. This construction is without seam allowances and can be used as a template to draft the patterns for fabric and interlinings. In this chapter we will demonstrate 3 important 2-piece collar forms for shirt collections:

- ☞ The classic "Kent" collar
- ☞ The "Button-down" collar and
- ☞ The "Shark fin" collar; with description of construction, interlining patterns, fabric patterns and fusing positions

It is the same principle of construction for all 2-piece collars, only forms and dimensions are different.

Collar band construction

We start drawing a basic construction line from centre back to centre front, a bit longer than the half neck measurement taken from the body pattern. At centre back we raise this point between 0.7 cm and 1.2 cm to draft the baseline of the collar band.

The fundamental rule is:

The more we raise the baseline; the more the collar band is curved and fits closer to the neck. The raised point at centre back is squared off (90°) and we draw the baseline of the collar band in a soft curve (as shown in the diagram), then we measure the half neck measurement along this baseline and get the centre front of the collar. We extend the collar band for the over wrap according to the width of front placket e.g. if the front placket is 3.5 cm wide (standard measurement), the over wrap is 1.75 cm wide. The over wrap is raised a few mm to fit the shape of the front neck hole.

Along the centre back line we measure the height of collar band (here 3.5 cm). This point is squared off (90°) and we draft the collar attachment line, as shown in the diagram. The collar band is tapered in towards the centre front, approximately 0.5 cm. Then we draw the collar nose as per design, e.g. round, with slanting corner or square.

Collar construction

Along the centre back line we take a gradient measurement (here 1.1 cm).

The fundamental rule is:

The higher the gradient measurement is, all the more the collar is curved and the collar outer edge is longer.

This point is squared off (90°) at centre back and we draw the collar attachment line to the collar band, as shown in the diagram. The collar flap is attached 2 – 3 mm behind centre front of collar band to get a tie-gap of 4 – 6 mm at centre front.

At the centre back line we measure the height of collar, which should be 0.8 cm to 1.1 cm more than the height of the collar band. This extra length is required to make the collar "roll" and to cover the neck seam at centre back; it is covered approximately 0.5 cm.

Then we draft the collar flap/point and the shape of the collar outer edge. The more the angle of the collar flap is positioned towards the front, all the closer is the distance of the collar points (collar spread).

The height of collar band and collar, the shape of collar baseline and collar outer edge, the angle of the collar flaps, the width of tie-gap, the collar spread (distance of collar points) and the choice of interlinings create the picture of a shirt collar, perhaps the most important component of a shirt.

Collar construction

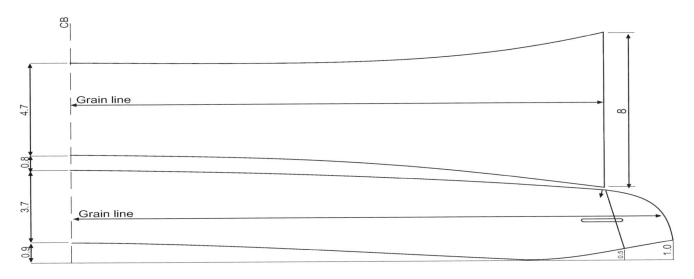

Construction Kent collar

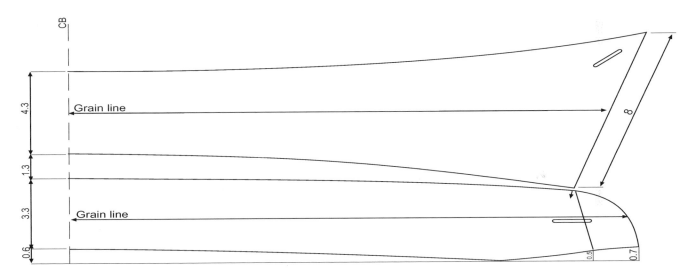

Construction button- down collar

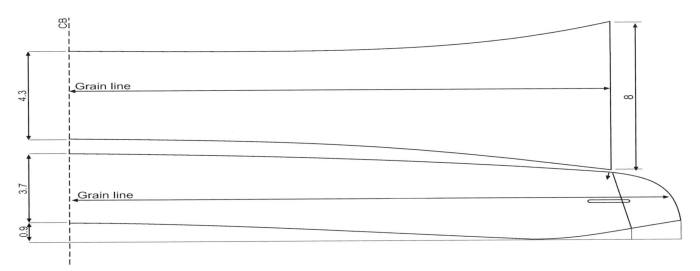

Construction shark fin collar

Collar construction

Constructions of interlinings

Collar

All collar forms have a basic interlining; it is cut 5 mm bigger than the finished collar dimension. It means that the interlining reaches 5 mm into the seam. The seam allowance for the fabric is 7 mm. For formal shirts with Kent, New Kent or Shark-fin collars the basic interlining gets an additional reinforcement interlining (collar patch). It is 1 – 2 mm smaller than the finished collar around the outer collar edge and 5 mm shorter at the collar attachment seam to the collar band, to make the rolling of the collar (break) possible.

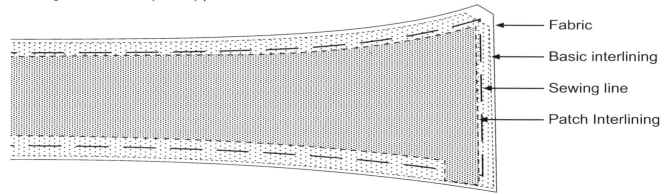

Interlinings for Kent collar

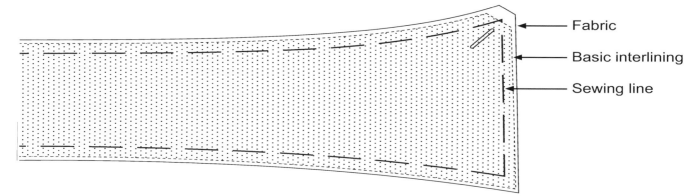

Interlinings for button- down collar. This collar has no patch

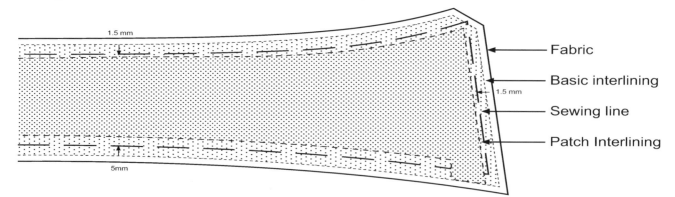

Interlinings for shark fin collar

Collar construction

Collar band

At the collar baseline and collar nose the interlining is cut net without extra allowance. At the collar attachment seam (collar is sewn to the collar band) the interlining is cut 5 mm above the sewing line (see detail drawing).

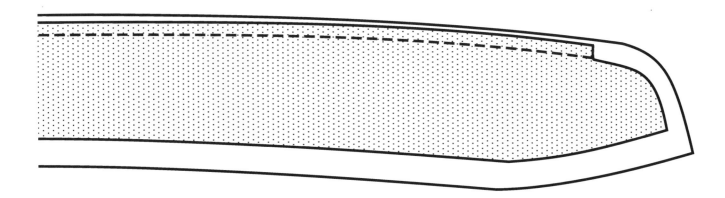

The ready made collars are looking as follows:

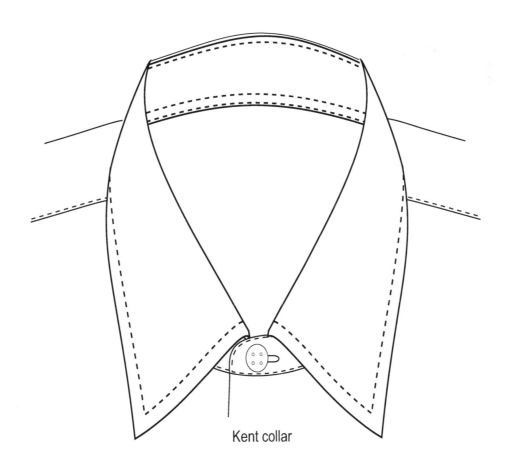

Kent collar

Collar construction

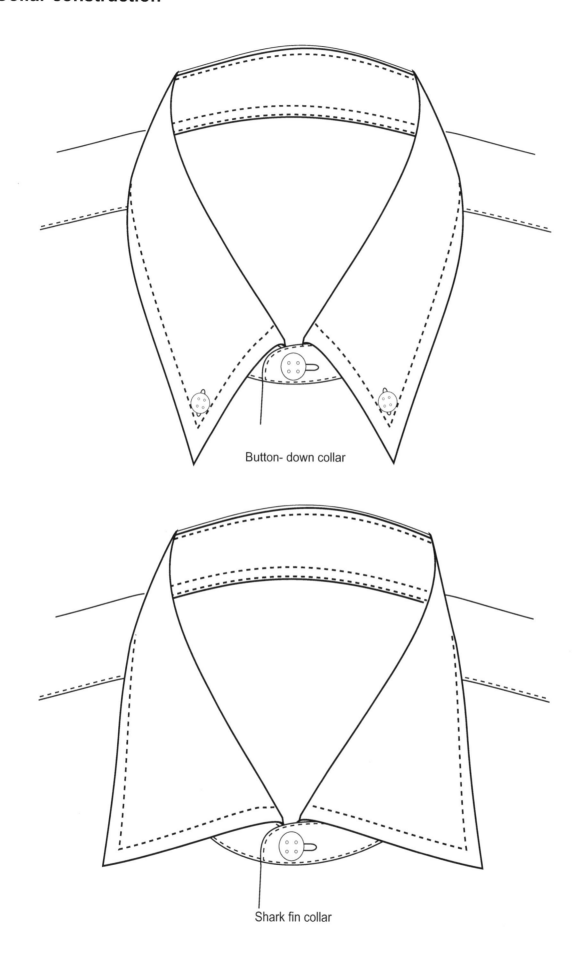

Button- down collar

Shark fin collar

Construction back parts

Construction back part

According form description and model analysis the back part is constructed and cut as follows:

- Plain back part without pleat
- Back part with two side pleats
- Back part with box pleat

Basic form is the construction without pleat. If pleats are demanded, the basic pattern part must be changed. The following drawings show the pleat space and the consumption of fabric is shown in grey.

All methods also work properly for a box pleat

Construction back parts

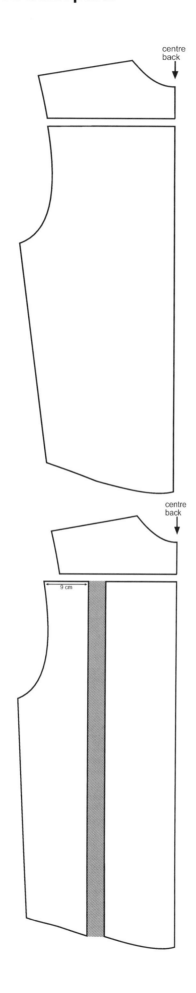

centre
back

centre
back

9 cm

Basic construction
See chapter pattern construction

Construction of side pleats opened through to bottom/hem line.
Here the back part is cut through approx. 9 cm from armhole and opened 2cm parallel. This is the easiest way to construct the pleat. The disadvantage is more width at chest, waist and hem line about 4 cm; the measurements don't correspondent with the measurement chart.

Construction back parts

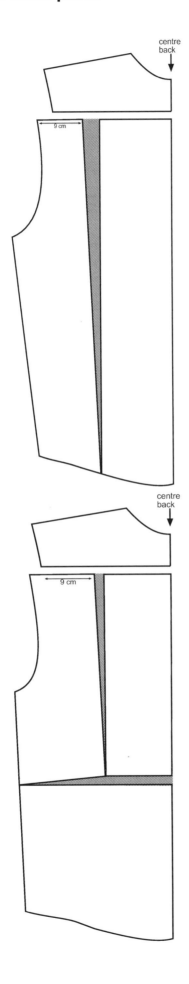

Construction with side pleat reduced to hemline.
Also here the back part is opened 9 cm from armhole, but not completely; at hemline the pattern is closed.
The waist is approx. 2 cm wider. The width at chest line is approx. 3.5 cm wider. The waist measurement does not correspond with measurement chart.

Construction with side pleat tapering off to waistline
This method takes the most effort but it is the best way to construct side pleats.
9 cm from armhole the back part is opended but only to waistline. Then the pattern is opened along waistline from centre back but kept closed at side seam. We get the space for the pleat, but waist and hip measurement is according to measurement chart. With this method the centre back length is approx. 0.6cm longer, which is in tolerance.

Section overview

Part 5 Design

The term "DESIGN" descends from the Italian word "disegno", meaning drawing, sketch and illustration. "Design" has become a synonymous word for drawings, sketches, drafts and model. In industry "Design" stands for styling and development of a product (garments, furniture, cars etc.). In previous parts of this book we explained details, patterns and manufacturing of standard shirts. But for casual, informal and fashion shirts creativeness has no limit, here we can play with forms and patterns. Many fashion trends are short-lived, they are "in today" and "out tomorrow"; while styling and silhouette changes little for classic and standard shirts. The right combination of many elements such as colour and patterns of fabric, the cut of material, accessories e.g. buttons, stitching details, embroidery or the form of collar, cuffs, front opening and pocket makes a good design and creates an interesting and attractive shirt.

The selection of design elements should always take into consideration "less can be more!"

It happens often that designers or merchandisers "go over board" and overdo the styling; then a man's shirt can look overloaded or even too feminine. Also practicality is a key point when designing a shirt e.g. 2 very small buttons at centre front of collar and complicated front or cuff buttoning may be interesting, but difficult to wear. A combination of different textures of materials or fancy buttons can create problems when washing the garment. For "iron free" and "easy care" shirts few seams and little topstitching should be used, and "safety seams" are better than "felled" or "lap" seams.

From a monetary point of view, bear in mind that many design features push up the selling price; the production price will be higher and the manufacturing time is longer e.g. if parts are embroidered or printed in another factory.

This chapter cannot pretend to completeness of this topic, there are too many varieties in form and styling. It should inspire your own creativeness and help you to select design elements for your collection.

Selecting the design element for a shirt

Selecting the design element for a shirt

Synopsis

Before choosing the details to design a shirt, one should consider the approriateness for the range. Some details are just not right!
The following tabulation shows which design elements are suitable for a particular shirt or which detail should not be used at all. It is not representative of completeness.

Term	Suitable elements	Non-suitable elements
Evening or Smoking shirt	Fine materials, e.g. fine cottons, silk; wing and classic Kent collar; fly fronts, pin tucks and pleated front panel; double cuffs with cufflinks and high class buttons.	Rough fabrics, tabs, pockets, asymmetric openings, prints or bold patterns.
Formal tailor and business shirt	Fine and elegant fabrics, discreet patterns and colours; Kent, New Kent and Shark fin collars, fold back and combi cuffs with cufflinks	Big patterns, strong colours, prints, bold embroidery, BD- collar, pocket flaps.
City dress shirt	Quality materials, solid colours, fine stripes, sometimes white colour and cuffs with rounded or cut corners; classic collars, discreet embroidery	Tabs, shoulder straps, big patterns, heavy prints, big buttons.
Semi-dress shirt	Solid fabrics, stripes and checks, small prints, stitching details, embroidery, small flags, Kent and BD-collar.	Silky fabrics, real mother-of-pearl buttons, covered fly front, wing, Shark fin and stiff New Kent collars.
Casual shirt, also crash and washer shirt	Fabrics with bolder stripes, checks and prints; top stitching elements, contrast stitching, flags and badges, tabs, interesting buttons, Kent and BD-collar.	Classic collars, e.g. New Kent and Shark fin, covered fly fronts, frills and pleats.
Fancy shirt	Fabrics in cotton, linen, viscose and mixed, with big patterns and fancy buttons, soft unconstructed collars.	Stiff interlinings, classic collars and cuffs.

Selecting the design element for a shirt

Costume shirt	Fabrics, cotton, linen and canvas, embroidery with flower and animal motif, badges and flags, tabs and roll up sleeves, special horn and metal buttons	Elegant materials, classic collars (Wing, Shark fin, New Kent.) turn back cuffs with cufflinks.
Uniform and service shirt	Shoulder flaps fixed with loop or small tunnel and button to show the rank of the wearer. The design has to follow service regulations.	
Working or guild shirt	The design has to follow traditional or business regulations.	

Selecting the design element for a shirt

Fabric

The fabric in quality, pattern and colour is perhaps the most important component of a shirt. High-class materials like silk, fine mercerized cottons, pure linen and cloth with special finishing e.g. "easy care" or "iron free" revalues the status and price of the shirt instantly. But shirts in these qualities will require special care and cleaning instructions.

While solid or discrete colours and plain weave fabrics are mainly used for classic and standard shirts, prints, yarn dyed woven stripes and checks and combinations of materials can achieve an impressive effect for semi-formal and casual shirts.

Here is an illustration for a border print
1 model of a short sleeve shirt, the print is placed in 4 different positions

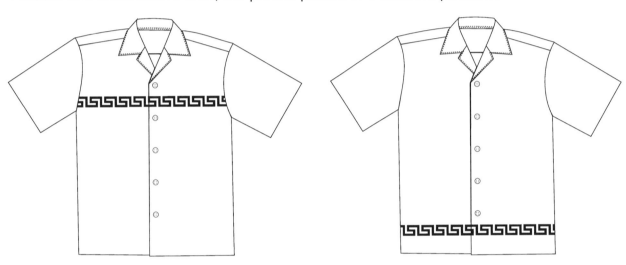

Print horizontal across front chest

Print horizontal across front part at hip level

Print vertical along middle of right front part

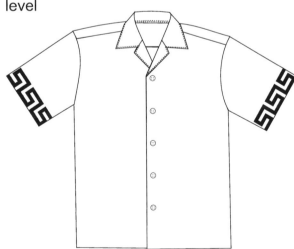

Print along hem / sleeve opening of short sleeve

Selecting the design element for a shirt

Front openings

There are many interesting design solutions for front plackets or openings. Previously we have explained the "Italian", "French", "Real placket" and "Covered fly front". But there are many more variations possible, see just a few styles below.

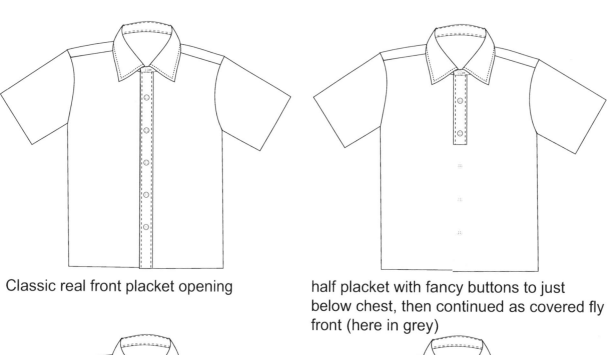

Classic real front placket opening

half placket with fancy buttons to just below chest, then continued as covered fly front (here in grey)

"John Wayne" inserted front opening

asymmetrical opening, also used for old uniform shirts

Selecting the design element for a shirt

A classic form of a man's shirt goes back, to when collar and cuffs were attachable to the shirt body. They could be replaced after being worn out and were mostly in solid, plain white fabrics. An update versision is this combination coloured shirt e.g. the body is grey or light blue in fil-à-fil or fine stripes, but collar and cuffs are in a white, plain weave fabric.

Form – grey shirt with white Kent collar and white rounded cuffs

Selecting the design element for a shirt

Cutting

Some front openings e.g. "John Wayne" shirt and split front plackets (1 half visible, the 2nd half covered) or frills, jabots etc. are out of fashion. Frills and pleats in front parts are still used for Evening and Party-shirts only. Increasing are special cuts like diagonal stripes (cut on bias), as already mentioned in chapter "Cutting"; but fabrics cut on bias will stretch in length and this can cause big problems in production e.g. slanting and puckering of seams, front placket and pocket.

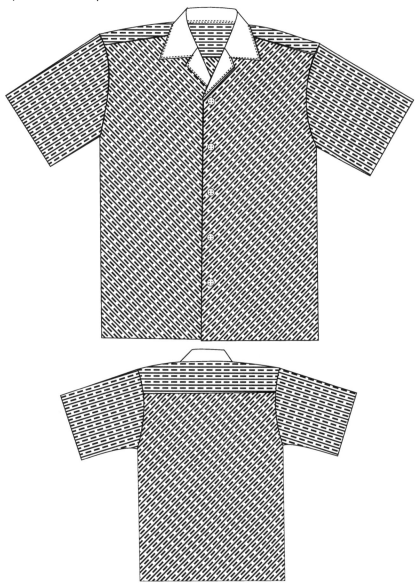

An example of a shirt cut on bias; here a casual shirt with short sleeves, one-piece collar and front facing in white fabric. Cutting: Back yoke and sleeves are cut straight; back part and fronts are cut diagonal – the front as "chevron".

Selecting the design element for a shirt

Collars

The collar is perhaps the main "eye-catcher" on the shirt and presents itself for many design ideas. Here are just some of many, e.g. a collar with extra high collar band, closed with 2 or even 3 small buttons at centre front (called "Italo Kent") or a double collar – the bigger under collar and a smaller top collar are in different fabrics – both collars are joined into one collar band.
Sketches 3 and 4 show collars where the collar spread (distance collar point to collar point) is pulled together and controlled by a fabric tab with press button (Tab collar) and a metal stick through stitched holes and fastened with small bolts outside on the top collar (Picadilly collar). The knot of a tie worn with Tab or Picadilly collar is pushed up and appears to be "padded".

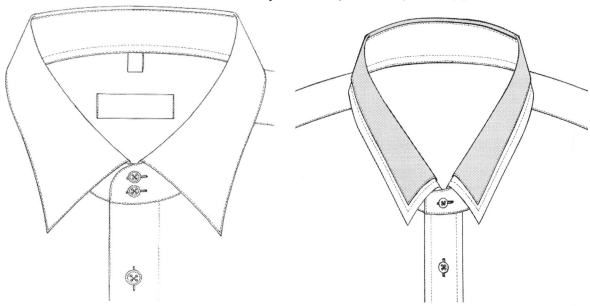

fashionable "Italo Kent" collar with 2 buttons

Double collar in two different materials

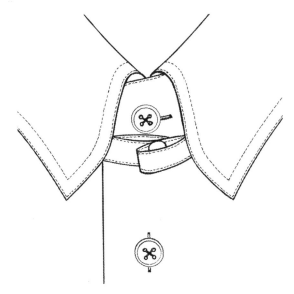

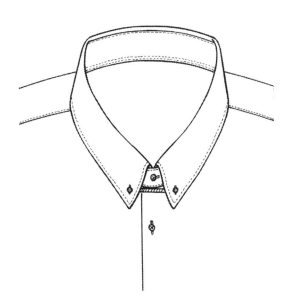

Tab collar with 2 loops and press button

Picadilly collar with metal stick

Selecting the design element for a shirt

Four ways to wear a Vario collar

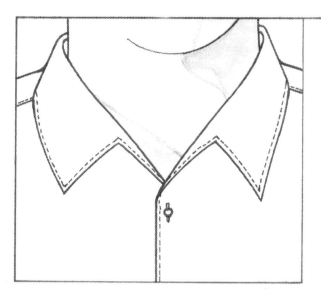

Worn open: casual and comfortable

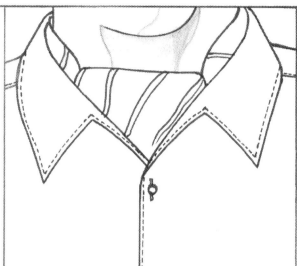

Worn with necktie: Elegant alternative

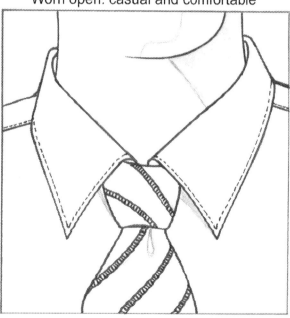

Closed tie: Perfect fit

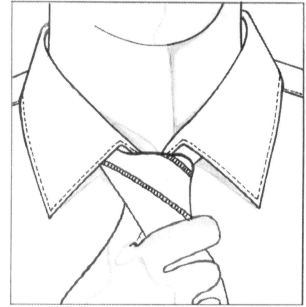

Tie slightly loose: Comfortable but still correct

Selecting the design element for a shirt

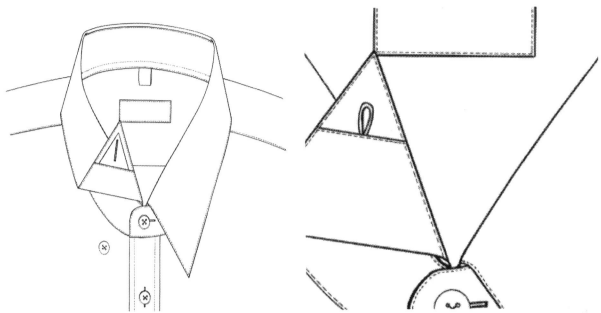

Under button-down collar with button hole   Under button-down with loop

Another interesting design idea is the "hidden button-down" collar. The collar is fastened to the front parts with small 14'" buttons. There are several possible constructions: a) a triangle tab with buttonhole out of an under collar seam; b) a fabric loop coming out of an under collar seam; c) a sewn pleat in under collar parallel to collar flap with buttonhole (here not illustrated).

The under button-down collar is fixed in position to the front parts, but the buttoning is not visible and the collar looks on top like a normal Kent collar.

Further collar variations are collars with removable collar sticks. The collar bones are not sewn in between top and under collar, but they are inserted into a channel on the under collar. The collar can be soft without the stick in the channel or correct with the collar bones inserted. Cutting and processing of these collars with removable collar sticks is difficult and more costly than sewn in collar bones.

What is said about collar design variations also applies to cuffs. There are extra deep cuffs with 2 or 3 buttons; cuffs with multi topstitching, laid on tapes or stitched pleats; "combi"-cuffs with buttons and suitable for cufflinks etc.

But keep in mind, the more complicated the styling is the more difficult is the handling and wearing this garment.

Selecting the design element for a shirt

Pockets

Chest pockets are also an endless range of design possibilities. As already mentioned in chapter "Cutting" pockets can be straight in grain line matching to front part or cut diagonal to fabric pattern; piping in contrast cloth or multi topstitching etc., there is no limit to design ideas. The same applies to pocket flaps for casual shirts.

In the following we illustrate just one pocket shape = a cut corner chest pocket, with different design variations. You can transfer this also to pointed pockets, pockets with round corners or straight corner pockets etc. We could design several hundred pockets without any hesitation.

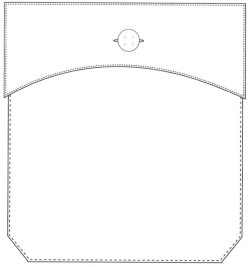

chest pocket with cut corners and with "half moon" shaped pocket flap, 1 button and horizontal buttonhole; as design variation could be 2 press buttons in the corners of the pocket flap.

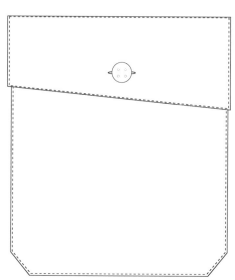

chest pocket with cut corners and with asymmetrical pocket flap (shorter to the front, longer at the side); 1 button and horizontal buttonhole

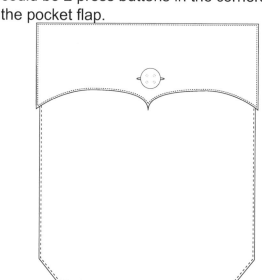

chest pocket with cut corners and with heart-shape pocket flap; often used for uniform shirts and American western shirts; 1 button and horizontal buttonhole.

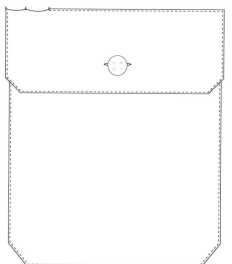

chest pocket with cut corners; worked as "pen-pocket" – there is an opening approximately 2,0 cm plus 1,5 cm on the left top side of the pocket flap, secured with bar tucks. These openings can hold pencils and ball point pens; 1 button and horizontal buttonhole

Selecting the design element for a shirt

Topstitching

Topstitching details are a simple but very effective element to make parts of a shirt more interesting. "Single", "multiple" or "stitching in contrast yarn", "zigzag" or "wavy" ornaments are easy for production, but they must be particularly controlled. The stitching lines must run even and without interruptions, joints of topstitching are not acceptable. Puckering must be avoided, machine tension and handling of the garment in sewing process has to be controlled constantly.

Examples of stitching details on a cut corner chest pocket without buttoning – one form in different variations

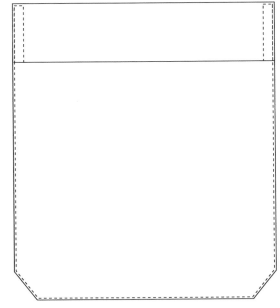

pocket with cut corners 1 mm stitched, pocket facing is double folded, but not hemmed

pocket with cut corners 1 + 5 mm twin needle or doubled stitched, double folded pocket facing not stitched through

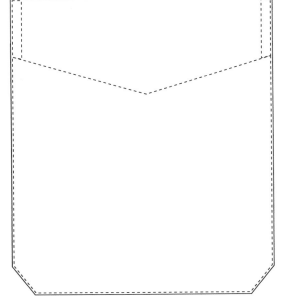

pocket with cut corners and pointed pocket facing, 1 mm stitched, facing stitched through

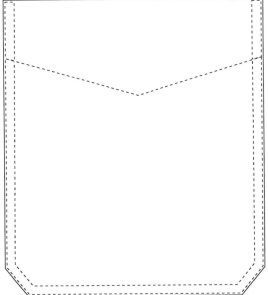

pocket with cut corners and with pointed pocket facing, 1 + 5 mm double stitched; pocket facing hemmed

Selecting the design element for a shirt

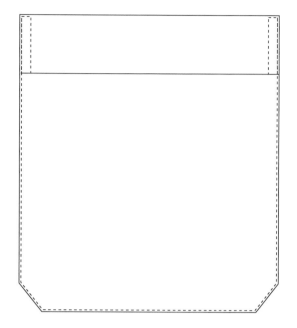

pocket with cut corners 1 mm stitched, straight pocket facing hemmed

pocket with cut corners,1 + 5 mm double stitched, straight pocket facing stitched through

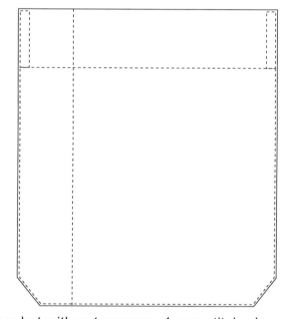

pocket with cut corners, 1 mm stitched, straight pocket facing hemmed; 3 cm from front edge of pocket a section through stitching separated with 1 buttonhole to hold pens etc.

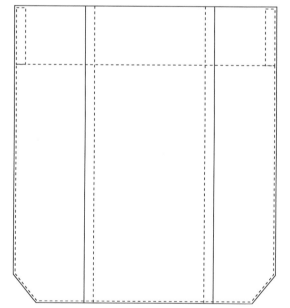

pocket with cut corners, 1 mm stitched, straight pocket facing hemmed; centre of pocket with 7 cm middle panel, 5 mm pleats sewn down at both sides of panel

Selecting the design element for a shirt

Buttons

Buttons are one of the most important accessories and can value to the shirt considerably. High-class buttons like real mother-of-pearl, real horn or tortoise-shell buttons make the shirt look precious and special. Of course their price is much higher and they are more difficult to handle in production than simple plastic shirt buttons. Some of these high quality buttons create problems when washing or cleaning the garment. For casual shirts and jeans wear press buttons (also called push- or snap-buttons) are an interesting alternative. The supplier must provide a certificate that any metal button, buckle etc. used is rust proof and nickel free to prevent allergic reactions to the end customer.

Embroideries

Embroideries give a special value to a shirt. Logos, names, motifs and ornaments can be embroidered. They should be placed clearly visible to catch the attention of the buyer. Embroideries are widely used for folklore and country style shirts with flower, animal, mountain, boots, feather and heraldic motifs. Embroideries are expensive and it takes special steps in production to get a good result. At first one has to design or develop the motif; then it has to be digitalized on a disk to operate the embroidery machine. There are a number of different machines on the market and it is important to find out about the right system which is used in the supplier's factory. The price for embroidery depends on number of stitches for the motif, how many colours and which yarn is used. The embroidery position has to be placed exactly on the pattern in 1:1 scale to adjust the embroidery machine and to mark the 1st stitch of the first needle. The material must be cut bigger to be stretched into an embroidery frame and under laid with fleece and embroidery interlining. These prevent the fabric being pulled together during embroidery process. Fleece and interlining must be removed after the embroidery motif is completed. Then the fabric should be ironed and the part (pocket, cuff, front placket ....) fine-cut.
If the shirt manufacturer has no embroidery facilities the pre-cut parts have to go to an outside embroidery firm; this might delay production time. Embroideries should be avoided on delicate and difficult materials.

Selecting the design element for a shirt

Following are few examples where the embroidery motif could be placed, here in form of a simple lily.

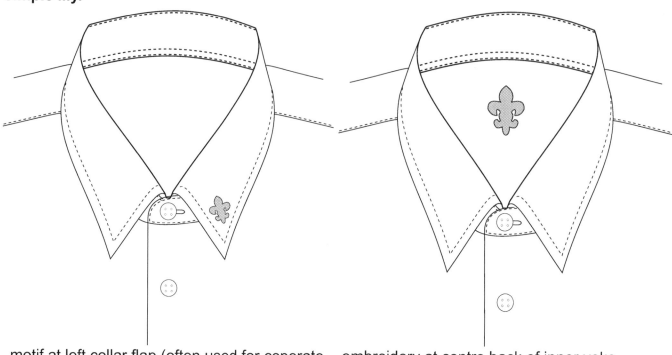

motif at left collar flap (often used for coperate identity of work garments)

embroidery at centre back of inner yoke

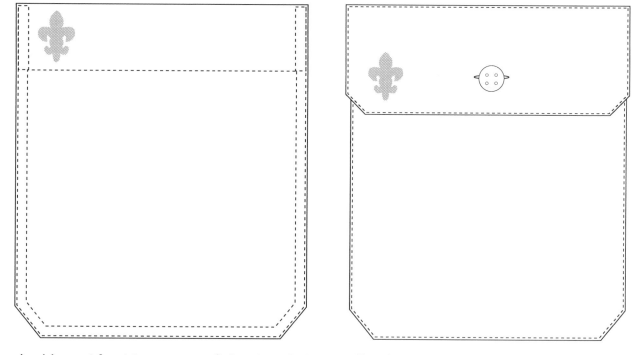

embroidery at front top corner of chest pocket

motif at front of pocket flap

Selecting the design element for a shirt

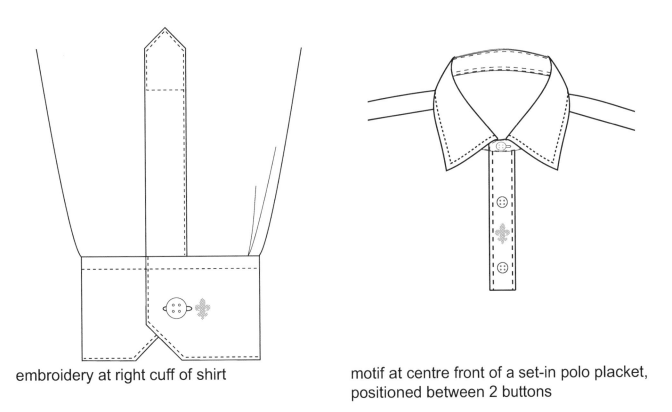

embroidery at right cuff of shirt

motif at centre front of a set-in polo placket, positioned between 2 buttons

Flags and "Laid ons"

"Flags" and laid on labels with logos or motifs can make a simple chest pocket more interesting and they are also used to promote the brand. Flags and labels can be inserted on patch pockets, pocket flaps, side seams … The possible variations are endless. Here just few examples of chest pockets and pocket flaps with straight pocket facing and different flag positions:

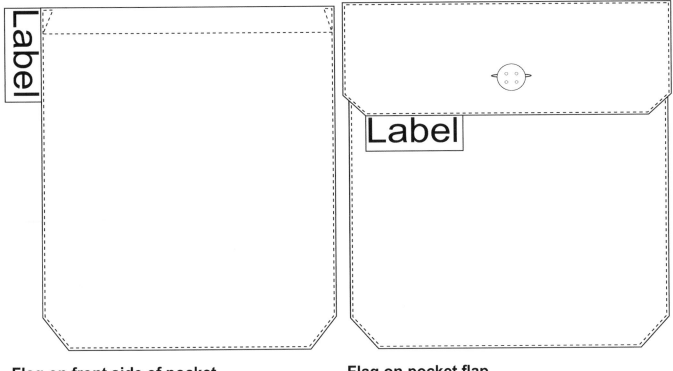

Flag on front side of pocket

Flag on pocket flap

Selecting the design element for a shirt

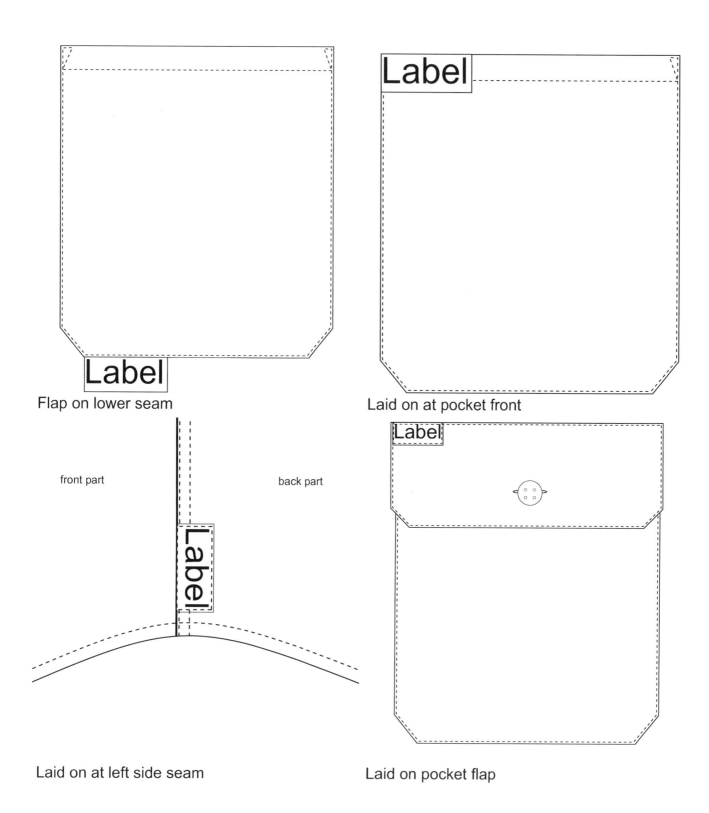

Flap on lower seam

Laid on at pocket front

front part

back part

Laid on at left side seam

Laid on pocket flap

Selecting the design element for a shirt

More design elements

Tabs and co

The use of tabs, loops or shoulder straps can create interesting details with simple means e.g. a loop over a box pleat at centre back yoke or a tab as in drawing below: a tab on the upper arm of sleeve to hold a roll-up sleeve. There are so many ways for tabs of roll-up sleeves e.g. the tab is attached at outer sleeve; or the tab comes out of inner sleeve and turned outside and fixed with a button on outer sleeve

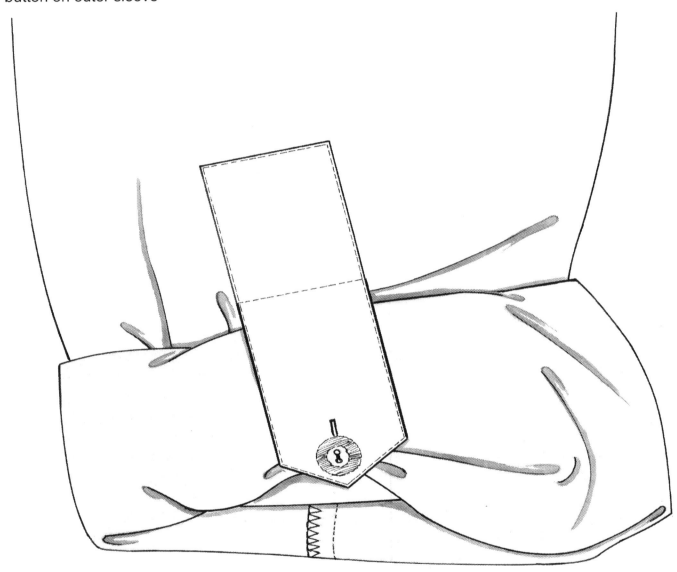

Selecting the design element for a shirt

Shoulder straps or Epaulettes

Specific service and uniform shirts must have a way to fasten badge or insignia of rank. Today's shoulder straps, also called "epaulettes", derived from rank ornaments fixed on the shoulders of 18 to 19th century uniforms. Epaulettes are still in use for military and pilot shirts and sometimes as design feature on casual and leisure wear shirts.

Here are 3 examples:

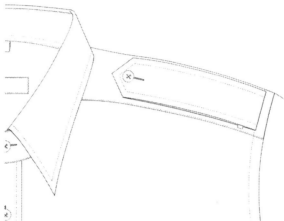

a double shoulder strap is pulled through a loop near the armhole and fastened with 1 button and 2 buttonholes on the shoulder

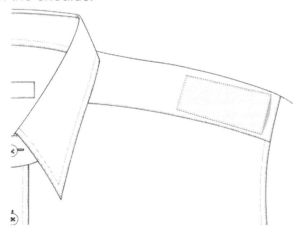

the epaulette with rank insignia is pulled through a tunnel on the shoulder

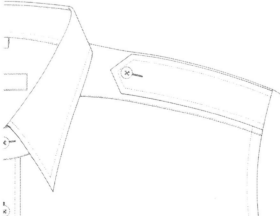

The shoulder strap is fixed inserted into armhole seam and fastened with button and button-hole on the shoulder. Rank badges can be pulled over the shoulder strap

Selecting the design element for a shirt

Sleeve openings on short sleeve

Besides a simple, straight hemmed sleeve ending, many interesting and varied forms are possible. It does not take considerable effort, but only some ideas for details. These designs should inspire, but will not claim to be complete.

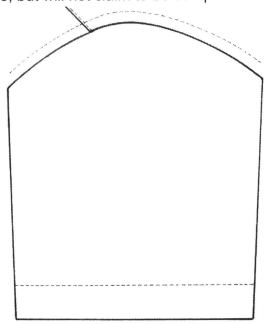

straight hemmed sleeve ending, 3 cm stitched

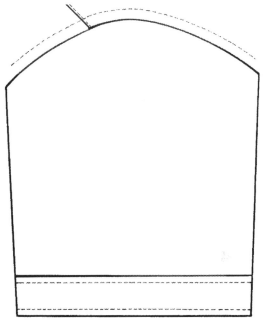

sleeve opening with 3 cm placket, 5 mm topstitching at top and bottom

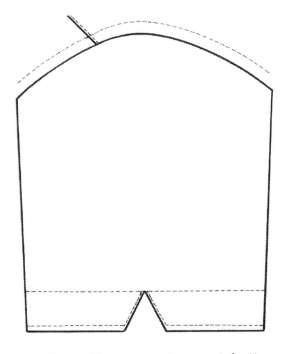

sleeve ending with sewn out gusset; bottom edge 5 mm topstitching, gusset 1 mm topstitching and hem 3 cm stitched

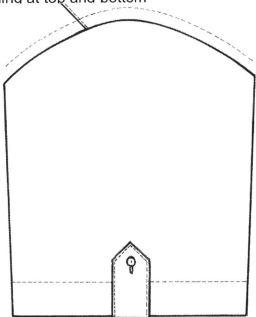

straight hemmed sleeve opening, 3 cm stitched; with pointed sleeve tab, small 14''' button and buttonhole

Selecting the design element for a shirt

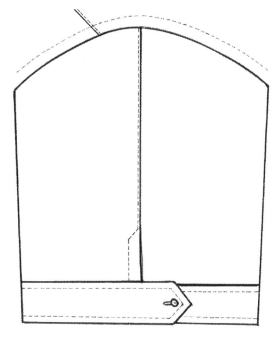

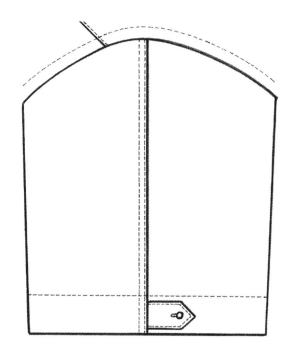

short sleeve with buttoned placket, stitched 5 mm all around; top sleeve seam 1 mm stitched, ending in a small 5 cm slit

straight hemmed sleeve ending, 3 cm stitched; top sleeve seam with double stitching 1 + 5 mm; 2,5 cm wide pointed tab with small 14''' button and buttonhole

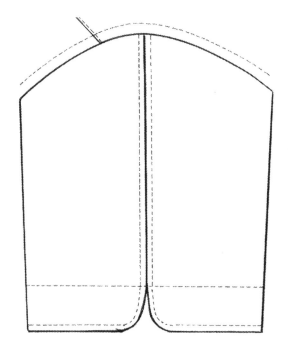

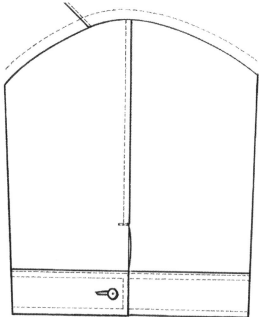

sleeve hem 3 cm stitched; top sleeve seam ending in curved hem line with 5 mm topstitching at both sides

sleeve ending with buttoned placket, 3,5 cm wide and 5 mm topstitched; placket worked like cuffs; top sleeve seam 5 mm topstitched ending in small 5 cm sleeve slit

Selecting the design element for a shirt

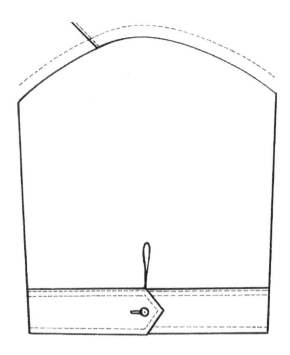

sleeve opening with attached placket, 3,5 cm wide and buttoned, 5 mm topstitching; small 5 cm piped sleeve slit

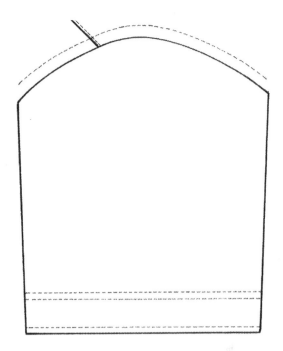

plain, straight hemmed sleeve ending, hem 3 cm wide, double stitched on top and 5 mm stitching on hem bottom

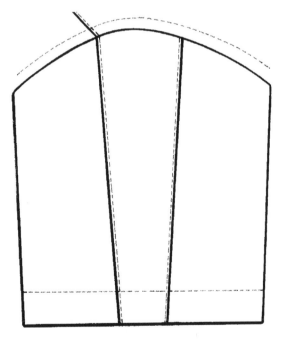

tapered, inserted panel 1 mm topstitched at both sides; hem 3 cm stitched

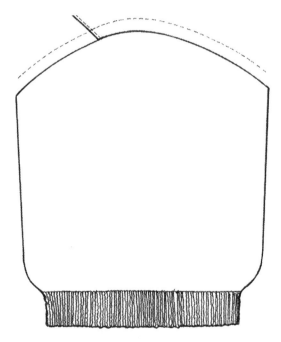

sleeve ending with 3 cm wide 1 x 1 knitted rib band

Part 6 Appendix

Retrospective historical view of the man's shirt

Already since the 3rd century A.C. a linen or sometimes woollen under dress was used in Central Europe. It had a comfortable wide cut and reached down to the upper thigh. This shirt-like garment was worn up into the 9th century. Natural and easy to wash materials became more and more popular, particularly as they were worn directly on the skin. This marked the beginning of the "shirt".

During the 12th century the shirt was ankle length and had two long side slits. But for physical hard working men the shirt was hip-level long and called "Niderkleit" (a medieval word meaning "under dress". The sleeves were long or short and sometimes enlarged through gussets (insets) at shoulder and armpit. In the second half of 14th century the man's shirt reached down to the upper thigh and the neck was visible at the scooped out neck line of the outer garment. After 1480 the shirt was extremely wide cut and the sleeves appeared through the slashed sleeves of the outer garment; so the shirt became an important part of fashion at the end of the 15th century. But it took a very long time until the shirt was widely and every day used.

During the 16th and 17th century shirts were opulent and decorated with lace, embroideries, pleats and pin tucks. Only the aristocracy and very rich citizens could afford it. During 18th century the man's shirt had a sewn out neck slit and a small stand-up collar, buttoned at centre front. Slit opening and collar were covered by a "Jabot" (a ruffled chest piece in lace) and a three-folded neck tie was worn around the stand-up collar. The tie was closed at the back with a buckle. Sometimes a cravat, the so called "Solitaire", completed the elegant outfit of a gentleman. For middle-class people the shirt was simpler and had a turn-down collar. After 1774 the shirt was worn open at the front and had the "Schiller" collar, a lay-out collar named after the German poet Schiller; it was the so called "Werther-Style", to express the enlightened mindedness of the wearer.

In 1804 the "jabot" came back but in reduced and simplified form. From 1840 on the jabot was only worn to complement an elegant evening shirt and dress-coat (tails); from now on a distinction was made in men's fashion between day-wear and evening outfit. In the first half of the 19th century a gusset was inserted at the shoulder and after 1850 also under the armpits.

1825 – 1835 a tight stand-up collar became fashionable, it was buttoned onto the shirt and turned-down. The collar was attached to a separate "chest or back pinafore". Because the collar was so tight and uncomfortable it got a special nickname in Germany, it was called "the parricide". A derivation of this collar is still used today in form of the "Wing-collar" for evening shirts. After 1850 the shirts were cut more fitted to the body, the straight side slits were rounded and separate stiff "Rolls" were buttoned on to replace the cuffs. In 1880 shirts with wing-collar came into fashion; they were complemented by "Tie" and "Plastron"; the outer garment was "Frock coat", "Cutaway" or "Jacket". After 1890 fancy coloured shirts became fashionable, but they had always a solid "white" collar.

The silhouette and cut of men's shirts changed little during the 20th century. The shape of the collar and later the fabrics were the main components for fashion.

1900 – 1910 stand-up and wing-collar were fashionable; but for informal shirts a turn-down collar with nearly parallel running collar flaps and double cuffs with cufflinks became more popular. Around 1910 silk shirts with soft, un-starched collars came into fashion, but the collar flaps and collar points were kept in shape with "Collar needles", sometimes "Fish bones" and later through "Plastic collar sticks". For casual shirts colourful materials were finally used.

Retrospective historical view of the man's shirt

From 1910 to 1922 the less starched "turn-down"-collar with rounded collar points was dominant; the "wing-collar" went out of fashion. This turn-down collar was popular for nearly 10 years.

In the 1930s colourful and patterned shirts became more and more popular, but the favourites were shirts with blue stripes and longer collar points. The fashion conscious "Dandy" did not close the collar button, but wore the collar open; it should look casual and "cool"!

Around 1930 – George Edward Alexander Windsor, "Duke of Kent" (1902 – 1942), the son of King George V of England, made a collar fashionable with collar flaps a little wider spread and collar points nearly in a right angle (90°), to allow space for a bigger tie-knot. Today this collar is dominant in any shirt collection and named after the Duke "KENT"-collar!

Around 1940 a leisure-wear shirt was designed, the so called "Bush-shirt", an "Africa-Safari" inspired shirt, worn with belt or loose without belt outside the pants. The material was Linen or Gabardine. The shirt featured a short "Slipon"- Revers –collar, four "Bellow"-pockets and short sleeves.

Between 1945 and 1950 shirts in darker colours were popular; sometimes with button-on attachable replacement collar and double cuffs.

1948 a casual, leisure-wear shirt became the "hit", the "Lacoste-shirt". René Lacoste was a French tennis player (winner of the Davis-Cup in 1927). In 1934 he designed a shirt suitable for the tennis sport with a triangular inset at the front neck.. This was replaced in 1950 by a short button placket ("Polo-placket"). This shirt is ever since known as "Polo-shirt". The soft fabric collar was later changed to a rib-knitted collar with wide spread (90°) collar points. The "Lacoste-logo" is world-wide patented, it's a "crocodile", mostly embroidered at the chest left front. The "Lacoste-shirt" is still very strong on the market; in different materials – mostly in cotton Piqué; it's an "evergreen".

Around 1950 the first easy care "Nylon-shirts" came from USA. They were in nylon fabrics, white, big cut and with Kent-collar. But there were some unpleasant side-effects wearing these shirts– heavy perspiration and body odour. Materials with high content of synthetic fibres are not much accepted by the consumer.

A younger fashionable collar for casual shirts turned up in the 1950s, the "Button-down collar". The collar points are fastened through 2 small 14''' buttons onto the front parts of the shirt. The Button-down collar is still widely used in all shirt collections.

About 1955 shirts with big diagonal stripes came into fashion; these patterns were called "Broadway-stripes".

In the mid 1950s men's shirts became even more colourful and manifold in shape and design. Tourism and travelling to exotic places was booming. There was the "Melbourne-shirt", the "Waikiki-shirt" and the "Titi-shirt" (all casual shirts worn over the trousers).

The "Melbourne-shirt" was specially designed for the Olympic Games 1956. The shirt had a deep front and back yoke with grown-on sleeves (like a yoke-kimono construction), a fold-down collar (similar as a "Vario-collar") and 2 big laid-on hip pockets.

The "Waikiki-shirt" is named after the famous "Waikiki-beach" in Honolulu. It is a high-summer leisure-time shirt with straight, comfortable cut, short sleeves, an open lay-out collar and several patch pockets. Typical were the large size and very colourful prints and patterns of the fabrics as known from the Pacific Islands.

Retrospective historical view of the man's shirt

The "Titi-shirt", also called "Titi-club shirt", was named after the famous Italian Men's Wear company "Trasformazioni Tessili" (in short form T.T. , pronounced TiTi). It was a casual summer-shirt with a horizontal neck line and a very wide spread turn-down collar. The Titi-shirt could not be worn with a tie because of the big front gap. It had colours without being "gaudy", often stripe fabrics; the shirt was worn over the pants.

1965 – 1975 The shirts were now slim fitted, underlining the figure. They had bigger collars with long collar points and simple, un-starched cuffs. Cottons, Linens and many mixed materials were the main fabrics used during this period.

In the mid 1970s the Italian stylist "C. Palazzi" designed elegant "Guru-shirts" in silk with high stand-up collars and zippers to close the shirt at centre back.

"Georgio Armani" presented in his collections high-fashion men's shirts with very low stand-up collars and the new small, cut-away and rounded "Armani-collar".

More and more knitted shirts, polo-shirts and T-shirts appeared on the market; they were easy to wear, relaxed and low in price. After 1975 until today (2006) men's shirts have a comfortable, straight or slightly fitted cut with Kent, Button-down, Shark-fin or Vario-collar. The patterns and colours are changing from season to season – from geometrical designs, to stripes, then checks, followed by prints etc.

2002 was the fashion year for an extra high collar with longer collar points. The collar band was closed with two , sometimes three small buttons; contrast buttonholes, occasionally slanted, were new details. This so called "Italo collar" was sold as Kent and Button-down collar.

The care of men's shirts

The care of men's shirts

The main reason for damage to textiles is not heavy or long usage, it is more a matter of bad care. Most shirts get care "until death". All textiles are stressed by washing with mechanic, thermal and chemical factors. To avoid early wear-out we give following care advice:

- If possible just use a colour saving detergent. Normal washing powder brightens colour or prints.
- Other substances like starch or conditioners harm fabric and environment and shouldn't be used.
- Program for washing should be "gentle care".
- Select temperature for washing according to care symbol or lower. (For example: 40 instead of 60 degrees.) Also with low temperature the shirts get clean and is saves energy.
- After washing short spin and put the shirt on a hanger for drying.
- The easiest way to iron a shirt is when moist. If too dry, take some water or steam. Temperature on iron must exactly follow care symbol to avoid stains or combustions to fabric.

The care of men's shirts

Care symbols

Care symbols give customers important information about how to care for their garments without irreversible damage of the product. The symbols and the correct order are standardized in ISO 3758.

Correct order of care symbols:

| Washing | Bleaching | Drying | Ironing | Professional cleaning |

Washing

The symbol for washing looks like a wash-tub. A number inside the tub shows the maximum temperature in which the fabric can be washed safely. The bar under the tub explains how gentle the washing process should be.

Temperature is 95 degrees celsius for normal processing

Temperature is 60 degrees celsius for gentle processing

Temperature is 30 degrees celsius for very gentle processing

Washing by hand only (e.g. wool)

Do not wash

In USA they don't use the temperature figures, just dots:

Cold   Warm   Hot

There are also bars underneath used for gentle ("Permanent Process") and very gentle processing.

The care of men's shirts

Bleaching

Any bleach allowed

Only oxygen or non-chlor-ne bleach allowed

No bleach allowed

There are also two older symbols which are not longer used in future:

Chlorine bleach allowed

No bleach allowed

Drying

The symbols for Europe inform only about drying with tumbler, the American symbols also give information about natural drying.

Tumble drying possible- low heat

Tumble drying possible

No tumble drying

In USA there are also bars underneath for gentle or very gentle drying.

The following symbols are used for natural drying

Drying general

Line dry

Dry flat

Drip dry

Dry in shade

Line dry in shade

Dry flat in shade

Drip dry in shade

The care of men's shirts

Ironing

Iron low, temperature max. 110° C

Iron medium, temperature max 150° C

Iron high heat, temperature max. 200° C

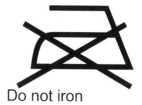

Do not iron

A special symbol for USA means: "Do not use steam while ironing."

Professional cleaning

The letter inside the circle informs which professional cleaning is possible. There are also bars for different cleaning processes.

Normal professional cleaning in Tetrachloroethylene or Perchlorethylene

Gentle professional wet cleaning

Very gentle cleaning in hydrocarbons

Do not dry clean

This older symbol means: All chemical substances can be used for professional cleaning, but it will not be used in future

This symbol means: No professional wet cleaning

Link list

Link list

In the last years we collected links to web sites, which are helpful for our work. This link list is stil-growing and won't be completed ever. We tried to provide the English version, but some sites are only available in their country language.

German business organisations

www.HDE.de
(Only German) The web site of the "Hauptverband des Deutschen Einzelhandels",a the leading organisation for German retailing.
www.bte.de
The website of "Bundesverband des Deutschen Textileinzelhandels. This site the page of German textile retailers.
www.twnetwork.de
Website of the leading German textile magazine "Textilwirtschaft"

German Chambers of Commerce

www.ahk.de/eng/index.html
German Chamber of commerce and their branches abroad
http://www.bdi-online.de/en/index_en.htm
The BDI – The umbrella Organization of German Industry
http://www.recycle-more.co.uk/
Helpful information for recycling and environment protection
http://www.gruener-punkt.de/?L=1
German Organisation for recycling

Further organisations

http://www.textile.fr
Umbrella Organization of French textile Industry
www.swisstextiles.ch
Organisation of Switzerland
www.textilindustrie.at
Organisation of Austrian textile industry
www.asstex.it
Organization of Italian textile industry
www.consejointertextil.com/
Organization of Spanish textile industry (Only in Spanish)
www.gzs.si/eng/
Slovenian organisation of textile industries
www.batc.co.uk/
British organisation
www.atmi.org
American textile manufacturers institute

Link list

CORPORATE SOCIAL RESPONSIBILITY

http://ec.europa.eu/employment_social/soc-dial/csr/index.htm
Website of the European Commission about CSR with links and other publications
http://www.oecd.org/department/0,2688,en_2649_33765_1_1_1_1_1,00.html
Website of the OECD about CSR, also with helpful links.
http://www.cleanclothes.org
A campaign to improve working conditions in the textile industry

Organisations for Standardization and proof

www.iso.org
The international leading organisation for other important national organisations:
www.din.de
Germany
www.bsi-global.com
UK
www.afnor.org
France
http://www.uni.com
Itali
www.on-norm.at
Austria
http://www.bsti.gov.bd
Bangladesh
www.sac.gov.cn
China
www.bis.org.in
Indian
www.tse.org.tr
Turkey
www.dssu.gov.ua
Ukraine
www.asro.ro
Romania
www.isrm.gov.mk
Macedonia
http://www.standards.org.au
Australia
www.ansi.org
USA
Other countries see hompage of www.ISO.org or www.google.com
www.hohenstein.de
The leading institute for proof in textile technology with branches in Turkey and China.

Linklist

Some important fairs and organisations

www.auma.de
Association of the German Trade fair industry with a big calendar of Germann fairs also abroad
http://www.igedo.com/IGEDO/index.php
Leading fair for men's wear in Düsseldorf
http://www.pittimmagine.com/en/fiere/filati/
Italian fair for fine fabrics
http://www.pratoexpo.com/newsite/english/intro.asp
Another important Italian fair.
http://www.premierevision-pluriel.com/
French fair for fabrics
http://www.expofil.com/en/home/home.php
Expofil in Paris
http://www.ifema.es/ferias/textilmoda/default.html
Textilmoda, the Spanish fair unfortunately only in Spanish
www.itf-its.com
Turkish leading fair for fabrics
http://www.messefrankfurt.com.hk/
This is an branch of German "Messe Frankfurt" in Hongkong.

All of these fairs have branches abroad here are only the mother companies.

Other helpful links

www.stofflexikon.de
A lexicon for fabrics and fibres

www.leo.org
A good online dictionary between Germann and English, French and Spanish
https://dpinfo.dpma.de/index_e.html
The information service from German patent and trade mark office. It helps to check if a trade mark is protected in Germany
http://en.wikipedia.org
The free encyclopedia that anyone can edit

Index

Index

Index

Index

Notes

Printed in the United States
206753BV00004B/4/A

9 783833 484889